PowerShell and WbemScripting

Working With Get

By Richard Thomas Edwards

CONTENTS

Sometimes you must take the good with the bad 5

How would you like your WMI? 13

Down at Downer's Gove 17

    Namespaces.vbs 18

    Categories.vbs 19

    Classes.vbs 21

The Many ways to use your WMI skills and impress people 27

Working with ASP 28

    For Single Line Horizontal 29

    For Multi Line Horizontal 31

    For Single Line Vertical 33

    For Multi Line Vertical 34

ASPX Code 37

    For Single Line Horizontal 37

For Multi Line Horizontal 39

For Single Line Vertical.. 41

For Multi Line Vertical 43

HTA Code.. 45

For Single Line Horizontal.. 45

For Multi Line Horizontal 47

For Single Line Vertical.. 49

For Multi Line Vertical 51

HTML Code... 53

For Single Line Horizontal 53

For Multi Line Horizontal 55

For Single Line Vertical 57

For Multi Line Vertical 58

Text Delimited File Examples.. 60

Colon Delimited 60

Comma Delimited 62

Exclamation 64

SEMI COLON 66

Tab Delimited.. 67

Tilde Delimited 69

THE XML FILES 72

Element XML... 72

WMI to Element XML For XSL.. 73

SCHEMA XML... 74

EXCEL 76

Using the comma delimited file 76

Excel Automation 78

Using A Spreadsheet 80

XSL 86

SINGLE LINE HORIZONTAL 87

For Multi Line Horizontal 88

For Single Line Vertical 90

For Multi Line Vertical 92

Stylesheets 94

Style sheets: 95

Stylesheets 100

NONE 100

BLACK AND WHITE TEXT 101

COLORED TEXT 103

OSCILLATING ROW COLORS 105

GHOST DECORATED 108

3D 110

SHADOW BOX 116

Sometimes you must take the good with the bad
This isn't one of them

am particularly excited about working with you. Not because you're about to buy this book but because I am about to share with you what I know about PowerShell!

It is truly an honor -- one of those unique times in my life – when I get a chance to be me and provide you with a book about learning PowerShell the way I learned PowerShell. And that was through trial and error – AKA the school of hard knots.

So, how did I learn PowerShell? Why should you want me to be in your wheelhouse guiding you though the rough seas of learning a language?

Simple, I learned PowerShell because it supported COM – Component Object Model – coding and I wanted to know as much as I could about the various programming languages which enabled me to write scripts using Windows Management Instrumentation or WMI. Between 2007 and now, being able to write scripts in the different scripting languages has kept me employed and enabled me to earn $65\hour.

So, I think the effort has paid off ten-fold.

Grabbing the coffee.

WHAT IS POWERSHELL

Here's my best way to describe it. It is a mixture of COM And .NET modules called cmdlets which provide administrators with a line by line console application. It is a mixture of VBScript and Perl Script.

VBScript:

```
Set l = CreateObject("WbemScripting.SWbemLocator")
Set svc = l.ConnectServer(".", "root\CIMv2")
svc.Security_.AuthenticationLevel = 6
svc.Security_.ImpersonationLevel = 3
Set objs = svc.InstancesOf("Win32_Process")
for each obj  in objs
    for each prop in obj.Properties_

    Next
    Exit For
Next
```

Perl Script:

```
use Win32;
use Win32::OLE('in');

$l = Win32::OLE->new("WbemScripting.SWbemLocator");
$svc = $l->ConnectServer(".", "root\\CIMv2");
$svc->Security_->AuthenticationLevel = 6;
$svc->Security_->ImpersonationLevel = 3;
$objs = $svc->InstancesOf("Win32_Process");
foreach $obj (in $objs)
{
  foreach $prop (in $obj->Properties_)
  {

  }
  last;
}
```

PowerShell:

```
$l = new-object -com WbemScripting.SWbemLocator
$svc = $l.ConnectServer(".", "root\cimv2")
$svc.Security_.AuthenticationLevel = 6
$svc.Security_.ImpersonationLevel = 3
$objs = $svc.InstancesOf("Win32_Process")
foreach($obj in $objs)
{
   foreach($prop in $obj.Properties_)
   {
      write-host $prop.Name.PadRight(30, " ")$prop.Value
   }
   break
}
```

Not too much of a difference here. Until you need to parse the values from the $property Names.

VBScript:

```
On Error Resume Next
Dim ns
Dim Classname
Dim v
ns = "root\Cimv2"
Classname = "Win32_Process"

Set locator = CreateObject("WbemScripting.SWbemLocator")
Set svc = locator.ConnectServer(".", "root\cimV2")
svc.Security_.AuthenticationLevel=6")
svc.Security_.ImpersonationLevel=3")
Set objs = svc.InstancesOf("Win32_Process")

For each obj in objs
```

```
    For each prop in obj.Properties_
        v=v + prop.Name & " " & getValue(prop.Name, obj) & vbcrlf
    Next
Next


WScript.Echo(v)

Function GetValue(ByVal Name, ByVal obj)

  Dim tempstr, pos, pName
  pName = Name
  tempstr = obj.GetObjectText_
  Name = Name + " = "
  pos = InStr(tempstr, Name)
  If pos Then

    pos = pos + Len(Name)
    tempstr = Mid(tempstr, pos, Len(tempstr))
    pos = InStr(tempstr, ";")
    tempstr = Mid(tempstr, 1, pos - 1)
    tempstr = Replace(tempstr, Chr(34), "")
    tempstr = Replace(tempstr, "{", "")
    tempstr = Replace(tempstr, "}", "")
    tempstr = Trim(tempstr)
    If obj.Properties_(pName).CIMType = 101 Then

      tempstr = Mid(tempstr, 5, 2) + "/" + _
            Mid(tempstr, 7, 2) + "/" + _
            Mid(tempstr, 1, 4) + " " + _
            Mid(tempstr, 9, 2) + ":" + _
            Mid(tempstr, 11, 2) + ":" + _
            Mid(tempstr, 11, 2) + ":" + _
            Mid(tempstr, 13, 2)
```

End If

    GetValue = tempstr

  Else

    GetValue = ""

  End If

End Function

Perl Script:

```perl
sub GetValue()
{

    local( $prop ) = shift @_;
    local( $obj) = shift @_;


    $N = $prop->{Name} . " = ";
    $tempstr = $obj->{GetObjectText_};
    $pos = index($tempstr, $N);
    if($pos > 0)
    {
       $pos = $pos .  length($N);
       $tempstr = substr($tempstr, $pos, length($tempstr));
       $pos = index($tempstr, ";");
       $tempstr = substr($tempstr, 0, $pos);
       $tempstr =~ s/{//gi;
       $tempstr =~ s/}//gi;
       $tempstr =~ s/"//gi;
       if($prop->CIMType eq 101)
       {
          if(length($tempstr) gt 13)
```

```
        {
            $tempstr = substr($tempstr, 4,2) . "/" . substr($tempstr, 6, 2) . "/" .
substr($tempstr, 0, 4) . " " . substr($tempstr, 8, 2) . ":" . substr($tempstr, 10, 2) .
":" . substr($tempstr, 12, 2);
            return($tempstr);
        }
      }
      else
      {
          return($tempstr);
      }

    }
    else
    {
        return("");
    }

  }
```

PowerShell:

```
function GetValue
{
   param
   (
   [string]$Name,
   [object]$obj
   )
   [string]$PName = $Name + " = "
   [string]$tempstr = $obj.GetObjectText_(0)
   $pos = $tempstr.IndexOf($PName)
   if ($pos -gt 0)
   {
      $pos = $pos + $PName.Length
      $tempstr = $tempstr.SubString($pos, ($tempstr.Length - $pos))
      $pos = $tempstr.IndexOf(";")
      $tempstr = $tempstr.SubString(0, $pos)
      $tempstr = $tempstr.Replace('"', "")
      $tempstr = $tempstr.Replace("}", "")
```

```powershell
      $tempstr = $tempstr.Replace("{", "")
      $tempstr = $tempstr.Trim()
      if($tempstr.Length -gt 14)
      {
         if($obj.Properties_.Item($Name).CIMType -eq 101)
         {
            [System.String]$tstr = $tempstr.SubString(4, 2)
            $tstr = $tstr + "/"
            $tstr = $tstr + $tempstr.SubString(6, 2)
            $tstr = $tstr + "/"
            $tstr = $tstr + $tempstr.SubString(0, 4)
            $tstr = $tstr + " "
            $tstr = $tstr + $tempstr.SubString(8, 2)
            $tstr = $tstr + ":"
            $tstr = $tstr + $tempstr.SubString(10, 2)
            $tstr = $tstr + ":"
            $tstr = $tstr + $tempstr.SubString(12, 2)
            $tempstr = $tstr
         }
      }
      return $tempstr
   }
   else
   {
      return ""
   }
}

$l = new-object -com WbemScripting.SWbemLocator
$svc = $l.ConnectServer(".", "root\cimv2")
$svc.Security_.AuthenticationLevel = 6
$svc.Security_.ImpersonationLevel = 3
$objs = $svc.InstancesOf("Win32_Process")
foreach($obj in $objs)
{
   foreach($prop in $obj.Properties_)
   {
      $value = GetValue $prop.Name $obj
      write-host $prop.Name.PadRight(30, " ")$value
   }
```

```
        break
    }
```

So, a lot of time and effort was spent on learning how to correctly parse out the values then in getting the core coding logic to work.

How would you like your WMI?

Async or Sync

ow, we're ready to go into interfaces that will help make this work to get the job done.

```
$l = New-object -com ("WbemScripting.SWbemLocator");
$svc = $l.ConnectServer(".", "root\\cimv2");
$svc.Security_.AuthenticationLevel = 6;
$svc.Security_.ImpersonationLevel = 3;
```

And you can use them in both Sync and Async mode.

Interface:

Get:

    Sync:

```
$objs = $svc.Get("Win32_Process", 131072);
```

Async:

> $mysink = New-object -com WbemScripting.SWbemSink")
>
> $svc.GetAsync($mysink, "Win32_Process", 131072)

The primary purpose of this is to find out if someone wrote a lengthy description on what the purpose of the $properties are and what the values those $properties mean. My experience with WMI tells me that most of the documented classes fall under the root\cimv2 namespace.

InstancesOf

Sync:

> $objs = $svc.InstancesOf("Win32_Process")

Async:

> $mysink = New-object -com WbemScripting.SWbemSink")
>
> $svc.InstancesOfAsync($mysink, "Win32_Process")

The primary purpose of this is to just get the information you want from the class without having to deal with an SQL or WQL query. It is the simplest to use and the workhorse of WbemScripting when you just want to glean the information from the class.

ExecNotificationQuery:

```
        $strQuery= "Select * From ___InstanceCreationEvent
WITHIN 1 where TargetInstance ISA 'Win32_Process'")


        $strQuery= "Select * From ___InstanceDeletionEvent
WITHIN 1 where TargetInstance ISA 'Win32_Process'")


        $strQuery= "Select * From ___InstanceModificationEvent
WITHIN 1 where TargetInstance ISA 'Win32_Process'")


        $strQuery= "Select * From ___InstanceOperationEvent
WITHIN 1 where TargetInstance ISA 'Win32_Process'")
```

Sync:

```
        $es = $svc.ExecNotificationQuery($strQuery)
```

Async:

```
        $mysink = New-object -com WbemScripting.SWbemSink

        svc.ExecNotificationQueryAsync($mysink, $strQuery)
```

This is the heart of many calls made through WMI to determine if an event has occurred that you want to know about. The ___InstanceOperationEvent is combination of all three. You just filter through the events to know if it is the one you are looking for and what type of event it is.

ExecQuery:

Sync:

```
$objs = $svc.ExecQuery("Select * From Win32_Process")
```

Async:

```
$mysink = New-object -com WbemScripting.SWbemSink
$svc.ExecQueryAsync($mysink, "Select * From Win32_Process")
```

This allows you to filter through all or some of the $properties that could be returned and query for a specific value.

Okay, so now that we have an idea of what we can do, let's start focusing on what the book uses.

Down at Downer's Gove
You want me to do what?

So, I'm up in Chicago working for Nuveen Investments and on the first day, I'm asked to make a VBScript to work that turns the network switch on the network adapter to go from LAN to a WAN connection. Confused?

Yep, so was I.

So, I'm thinking, first day on the job and I'm being given a sink or swim assignment. No pressure.

Turns out, it took me about 30 minutes to get it to work, everyone was happy, and I stayed gainfully employed for the next 9 months. So, what's the point?

Unless you know what the classes, where to find them and what they are capable of, there is no way you can intelligently work. With that said, below are three scripts – I wrote these what seems like a million years ago – that will tell you as well as profile for you each namespace and class that is on your machine.

You should use the same naming conventions I used as well as place them into the same directory. I like creating a folder on the desktop and calling it WMI Directory, but you can create it anywhere and it anything you want.

Namespaces.vbs

```
Dim fso
Dim l
Dim s


EnumNamespaces("root")


Sub EnumNamespaces(ByVal nspace)

Set ws = createobject("Wscript.Shell
Set fso = CreateObject("Scripting.FilesystemObject

If fso.folderExists(ws.currentDirectory & "\" & nspace) = false then
 fso.CreateFolder(ws.currentDirectory & "\" & nspace)
End If

On error Resume Next

Set objs = GetObject("Winmgmts:\\.\" &
nspace).InstancesOf("___Namespace", &H20000)

If err.Number <> 0 Then
  err.Clear
  Exit Sub
End If

For each obj in objs

   EnumNamespaces(nspace & "\" & obj.Name)
Next
```

```
End Sub
```

Categories.vbs

```
Dim fso
Dim l
Dim s

Set ws = createobject("Wscript.Shell
Set fso = CreateObject("Scripting.FilesystemObject

EnumNamespaces("root")


Sub EnumNamespaces(ByVal nspace)

EnumCategories(nspace)

If fso.folderExists(ws.currentDirectory & "\" & nspace) = false then
 fso.CreateFolder(ws.currentDirectory & "\" & nspace)
End If

On error Resume Next

Set objs = GetObject("Winmgmts:\\.\" &
nspace).InstancesOf("___Namespace", &H20000)

If err.Number <> 0 Then
  err.Clear
  Exit Sub
End If
```

```
For each obj in objs

    EnumNamespaces(nspace & "\" & obj.Name)

Next

End Sub

Sub EnumCategories(ByVal nspace)

Set ws = createobject("Wscript.Shell
Set fso = CreateObject("Scripting.FilesystemObject

Set objs = GetObject("Winmgmts:\\.\" & nspace).SubClassesOf("", &H20000)
For each obj in objs

    pos = instr(obj.Path_.class, "_")

    if pos = 0 then
        If fso.folderExists(ws.currentDirectory & "\" & nspace & "\" &
obj.Path_.Class) = false then
            fso.CreateFolder(ws.currentDirectory & "\" & nspace & "\" &
obj.Path_.Class)
        End If
    else
        if pos = 1 then
            If fso.folderExists(ws.currentDirectory & "\" & nspace &
"\SuperClasses") = false then
                fso.CreateFolder(ws.currentDirectory & "\" & nspace &
"\SuperClasses")
            End If
        else
```

```
            If fso.folderExists(ws.currentDirectory & "\" & nspace & "\" &
Mid(obj.Path_.Class, 1, pos-1)) = false then
                fso.CreateFolder(ws.currentDirectory & "\" & nspace & "\" &
Mid(obj.Path_.Class, 1, pos-1))
            End If
        End If
      End If


    Next


    End Sub
```

Classes.vbs

```
    Dim fso
    Dim l
    Dim s

    EnumNamespaces("root")

    Sub EnumNamespaces(ByVal nspace)

    EnumClasses(nspace)

    Set ws = createobject("Wscript.Shell
    Set fso = CreateObject("Scripting.FilesystemObject

    If fso.folderExists(ws.currentDirectory & "\" & nspace) = false then
     fso.CreateFolder(ws.currentDirectory & "\" & nspace)
    End If

    On error Resume Next
```

```
    Set objs = GetObject("Winmgmts:\\.\" &
nspace).InstancesOf("___Namespace", &H20000)

    If err.Number <> 0 Then
      err.Clear
      Exit Sub
    End If

    For each obj in objs

       EnumNamespaces(nspace & "\" & obj.Name)

    Next

    End Sub

    Sub EnumClasses(ByVal nspace)

    Set ws = createobject("Wscript.Shell
    Set fso = CreateObject("Scripting.FilesystemObject

    Set objs = GetObject("Winmgmts:\\.\" & nspace).SubClassesOf("", &H20000)
    For each obj in objs

       pos = instr(obj.Path_.class, "_")

      if pos = 0 then
          CreateXMLFile(ws.CurrentDirectory & "\" & nspace & "\" &
obj.Path_.Class, nspace, obj.Path_.Class)
        else
         if pos = 1 then
            CreateXMlFile(ws.CurrentDirectory & "\" & nspace & "\Superclasses",
nspace, obj.Path_.Class)
```

```
            else
                CreateXMLFile(ws.CurrentDirectory & "\" & nspace & "\" &
Mid(obj.Path_.Class, 1, pos-1), nspace, obj.Path_.Class)
            End If
        End If


    Next


End Sub


Sub CreateXMLFile(ByVal Path, ByVal nspace, ByVal ClassName)



    Set fso = CreateObject("Scripting.FileSystemObject
    Dim shorty
    On error Resume Next
    shorty = fso.GetFolder(Path).ShortPath
    If err.Number <> 0 then
    err.Clear
    Exit Sub
    End IF



    set obj = GetObject("Winmgmts:\\.\" & nspace).Get(classname)


    Set txtstream = fso.OpenTextFile(Shorty & "\" & Classname & ".xml", 2, $true,
-2)
    txtstream.WriteLine("<data>")
    txtstream.WriteLine("  <NamespaceInformation>")
    txtstream.WriteLine("    <namespace>" & nspace & "</namespace>")
    txtstream.WriteLine("    <classname>" & classname & "</classname>")
    txtstream.WriteLine("  </NamespaceInformation>")
```

23

```
txtstream.WriteLine("  <properties>")

    for each prop in obj.Properties_
        txtstream.WriteLine("    <property Name = """ & prop.Name & """
IsArray=""" & prop.IsArray & """ DataType = """ &
prop.Qualifiers_("CIMType").Value & """/>")
    Next
    txtstream.WriteLine("  </properties>")
    txtstream.WriteLine("</data>")
    txtstream.close

End sub
```

Copy and paste these into Notepad and save them in the new folder you just created. Run Namespaces.vbs first. Then Categories.vbs and finally, Classes.vbs.

The last one could take a while. Perhaps 7 to 10 minutes. When it is done. Click on the root folder and then CIMV2 folder. Look for Win32 folder and open it.

You should see a similar display as shown on the next page.

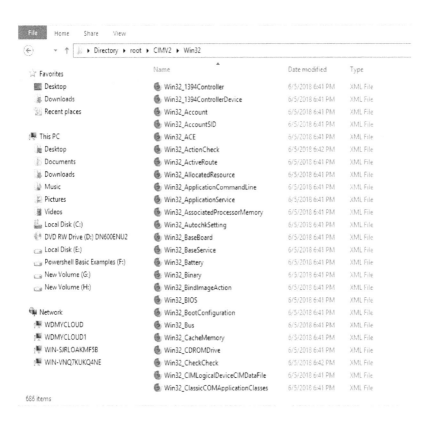

And If you open one of these up:

- <data>
  - <NamespaceInformation>
      <namespace>root\CIMV2</namespace>
      <classname>Win32_BIOS</classname>
    </NamespaceInformation>
  - <properties>
      <property Name="BiosCharacteristics" IsArray="True" DataType="uint16"/>
      <property Name="BIOSVersion" IsArray="True" DataType="string"/>
      <property Name="BuildNumber" IsArray="False" DataType="string"/>
      <property Name="Caption" IsArray="False" DataType="string"/>
      <property Name="CodeSet" IsArray="False" DataType="string"/>
      <property Name="CurrentLanguage" IsArray="False" DataType="string"/>
      <property Name="Description" IsArray="False" DataType="string"/>
      <property Name="IdentificationCode" IsArray="False" DataType="string"/>
      <property Name="InstallableLanguages" IsArray="False" DataType="uint16"/>
      <property Name="InstallDate" IsArray="False" DataType="datetime"/>
      <property Name="LanguageEdition" IsArray="False" DataType="string"/>
      <property Name="ListOfLanguages" IsArray="True" DataType="string"/>
      <property Name="Manufacturer" IsArray="False" DataType="string"/>
      <property Name="Name" IsArray="False" DataType="string"/>
      <property Name="OtherTargetOS" IsArray="False" DataType="string"/>
      <property Name="PrimaryBIOS" IsArray="False" DataType="boolean"/>
      <property Name="ReleaseDate" IsArray="False" DataType="datetime"/>
      <property Name="SerialNumber" IsArray="False" DataType="string"/>
      <property Name="SMBIOSBIOSVersion" IsArray="False" DataType="string"/>
      <property Name="SMBIOSMajorVersion" IsArray="False" DataType="uint16"/>
      <property Name="SMBIOSMinorVersion" IsArray="False" DataType="uint16"/>
      <property Name="SMBIOSPresent" IsArray="False" DataType="boolean"/>
      <property Name="SoftwareElementID" IsArray="False" DataType="string"/>
      <property Name="SoftwareElementState" IsArray="False" DataType="uint16"/>
      <property Name="Status" IsArray="False" DataType="string"/>
      <property Name="TargetOperatingSystem" IsArray="False" DataType="uint16"/>
      <property Name="Version" IsArray="False" DataType="string"/>
    </properties>
  </data>

The Many ways to use your WMI skills and impress people

The following is list of the what we're going to be using with WMI:

ASP

ASPX

Attribute XML

Delimited Files

Element XML

Element XML For XSL

Excel

HTA

HTML

Schema XML

XSL

I need to do this before someone complains.

Up to here, the various languages I'm going to cover will have the same chapters. But past here, the code is specifically for each language. All will have the same code examples but written in the language specified in the title.

Working with ASP
The concept of programs writing programs

I NEED TO SHARE SOMETHING IMPOTANT WITH YOU THAT I HAVE SEEN ASKED BY PROS OVER AND OVER AGAIN. THE FACT THAT THEY ARE ASKING IT SHOWS JUST HOW UNAWARE THEY ARE OF THIS IMPORTANT FACT.

Anything you write inside a textstream is considered by the compiler to be a string and not code.

So, if I type:

For VBScript, VB, VBS, VB.Net, Python, Ruby:
$txtstream.WriteLine("Response.Write(""<tr>""" & vbcrlf) ")
For Javascript, JScript:
$txtstream.WriteLine("Response.Write(""<tr>""" & vbcrlf) ")
For Kixtart:
$txtstream.WriteLine("Response.Write(""<tr>""" & vbcrlf) ")
For C#:
$txtstream.WriteLine("Response.Write(\"<tr>\" & vbcrlf) ")
For C. . :
txtstream.WriteLine("Response.Write(\"<tr>\" & vbcrlf) ")
For PowerShell:
$txtstream.WriteLine("Response.Write(""<tr>""" & vbcrlf) ")

For Rexx:

txtstream~WriteLine("Response.Write(""<tr>"" & vbcrlf) ")

For Borland C Builder:

txtstream.OLEFunction("WriteLine", OleVariant("Response.Write(""<tr>"" & vbcrlf) ")

For Borland Delphi:

$txtstream.WriteLine('Response.Write(''<tr> '' & vbcrlf) ')

Aside from conforming to the compiler's expectations for single and double quotes, see any difference in the Response.Write("<tr>" & vbcrlf). It's because that part of the code is written to run as VBScript.

That also means any of the 14 languages listed could also create any of the other 14 languages. Hence, Programs that write programs. Below, is the code for ASP. The getValue function is in Appendix B.

```
$l = New-object -com WbemScripting.SWbemLocator
$svc = $l.ConnectServer(".", "root\\cimv2")
$svc.Security_.AuthenticationLevel=6")
$svc.Security_.ImpersonationLevel=3")

$ob = $svc.Get("Win32_Process")
$objs = $ob.Instances_(0)

$ws = New-object -com WScript.Shell
$txtstream = $fso.OpenTextFile($ws.CurrentDirectory .
"\\Win32_Process.asp", 2, $true, -2)
```

For Single Line Horizontal

```
$txtstream.WriteLine("<html>")
$txtstream.WriteLine("<head>")
$txtstream.WriteLine("<style type='text/css'>")
```

```
$txtstream.WriteLine("th")
$txtstream.WriteLine("{")
$txtstream.WriteLine("    COLOR: darkred;")
$txtstream.WriteLine("    BACKGROUND-COLOR: white;")
$txtstream.WriteLine("    FONT-FAMILY:font-family: Cambria, serif;")
$txtstream.WriteLine("    FONT-SIZE: 12px;")
$txtstream.WriteLine("    text-align: left;")
$txtstream.WriteLine("    white-Space: nowrap;")
$txtstream.WriteLine("}")
$txtstream.WriteLine("td")
$txtstream.WriteLine("{")
$txtstream.WriteLine("    COLOR: navy;")
$txtstream.WriteLine("    BACKGROUND-COLOR: white;")
$txtstream.WriteLine("    FONT-FAMILY: font-family: Cambria, serif;")
$txtstream.WriteLine("    FONT-SIZE: 12px;")
$txtstream.WriteLine("    text-align: left;")
$txtstream.WriteLine("    white-Space: nowrap;")
$txtstream.WriteLine("}")
$txtstream.WriteLine("</style>")
$txtstream.WriteLine("<title>Win32_Process</title>")
$txtstream.WriteLine("</head>")
$txtstream.WriteLine("<body>")
```

Use this if you want to create a border around your table:
```
$txtstream.WriteLine("<table Border='1' cellpadding='1' cellspacing='1'>")
```

Use this if you don't want to create a border around your table:
```
$txtstream.WriteLine("<table Border='0' cellpadding='1' cellspacing='1'>")
```

```
$txtstream.WriteLine("<%")
$obj = $objs.ItemIndex(0)
$txtstream.WriteLine("Response.Write(""<tr>"" & vbcrlf)")
foreach($prop in $obj.Properties_)
```

```
    {
        $txtstream.WriteLine("Response.Write(""<th>" + $prop.Name + "</th>"" &
vbcrlf)")
    }
    $txtstream.WriteLine("Response.Write(""</tr>"" & vbcrlf)")
    $txtstream.WriteLine("Response.Write(""<tr>"" & vbcrlf)")

    foreach($prop in $obj.Properties_)
    {
        $txtstream.WriteLine("Response.Write(""<td>" + GetValue($prop.Name,
$obj) + "</td>"" & vbcrlf)")
    }
    $txtstream.WriteLine("Response.Write(""</tr>"" & vbcrlf)")
    $txtstream.WriteLine("%>")
    $txtstream.WriteLine("</table>")
    $txtstream.WriteLine("</body>")
    $txtstream.WriteLine("</html>")
    $txtstream.Close()
```

For Multi Line Horizontal

```
    $txtstream.WriteLine("<html>")
    $txtstream.WriteLine("<head>")
    $txtstream.WriteLine("<style type='text/css'>")
    $txtstream.WriteLine("th")
    $txtstream.WriteLine("{")
    $txtstream.WriteLine("    COLOR: darkred;")
    $txtstream.WriteLine("    BACKGROUND-COLOR: white;")
    $txtstream.WriteLine("    FONT-FAMILY:font-family: Cambria, serif;")
    $txtstream.WriteLine("    FONT-SIZE: 12px;")
    $txtstream.WriteLine("    text-align: left;")
    $txtstream.WriteLine("    white-Space: nowrap;")
    $txtstream.WriteLine("}")
```

```
$txtstream.WriteLine("td")
$txtstream.WriteLine("{")
$txtstream.WriteLine("    COLOR: navy;")
$txtstream.WriteLine("    BACKGROUND-COLOR: white;")
$txtstream.WriteLine("    FONT-FAMILY: font-family: Cambria, serif;")
$txtstream.WriteLine("    FONT-SIZE: 12px;")
$txtstream.WriteLine("    text-align: left;")
$txtstream.WriteLine("    white-Space: nowrap;")
$txtstream.WriteLine("}")
$txtstream.WriteLine("</style>")
$txtstream.WriteLine("<title>Win32_Process</title>")
$txtstream.WriteLine("</head>")
$txtstream.WriteLine("<body>")
```

Use this if you want to create a border around your table:

```
$txtstream.WriteLine("<table Border='1' cellpadding='1' cellspacing='1'>")
```

Use this if you don't want to create a border around your table:

```
$txtstream.WriteLine("<table Border='0' cellpadding='1' cellspacing='1'>")
```

```
$txtstream.WriteLine("<%")
$obj = $objs.ItemIndex(0)
$txtstream.WriteLine("Response.Write(""<tr>"" & vbcrlf)")
foreach($prop in $obj.Properties_)
{
    $txtstream.WriteLine("Response.Write(""<th>" + $prop.Name + "</th>"" & vbcrlf)")
}
$txtstream.WriteLine("Response.Write(""</tr>"" & vbcrlf)")
foreach($obj in $objs)
{
    $txtstream.WriteLine("Response.Write(""<tr>"" & vbcrlf)")
    foreach($prop in $obj.Properties_)
```

```
        {
            $txtstream.WriteLine("Response.Write(""<td>" + GetValue($prop.Name,
$obj) + "</td>""" & vbcrlf)")
        }
        $txtstream.WriteLine("Response.Write(""</tr>""" & vbcrlf)")
    }
    $txtstream.WriteLine("%>")
    $txtstream.WriteLine("</table>")
    $txtstream.WriteLine("</body>")
    $txtstream.WriteLine("</html>")
    $txtstream.Close()
```

For Single Line Vertical

```
    $txtstream.WriteLine("<html>")
    $txtstream.WriteLine("<head>")
    $txtstream.WriteLine("<style type='text/css'>")
    $txtstream.WriteLine("th")
    $txtstream.WriteLine("{")
    $txtstream.WriteLine("   COLOR: darkred;")
    $txtstream.WriteLine("   BACKGROUND-COLOR: white;")
    $txtstream.WriteLine("   FONT-FAMILY:font-family: Cambria, serif;")
    $txtstream.WriteLine("   FONT-SIZE: 12px;")
    $txtstream.WriteLine("   text-align: left;")
    $txtstream.WriteLine("   white-Space: nowrap;")
    $txtstream.WriteLine("}")
    $txtstream.WriteLine("td")
    $txtstream.WriteLine("{")
    $txtstream.WriteLine("   COLOR: navy;")
    $txtstream.WriteLine("   BACKGROUND-COLOR: white;")
    $txtstream.WriteLine("   FONT-FAMILY: font-family: Cambria, serif;")
    $txtstream.WriteLine("   FONT-SIZE: 12px;")
    $txtstream.WriteLine("   text-align: left;")
    $txtstream.WriteLine("   white-Space: nowrap;")
```

```
$txtstream.WriteLine("}")
$txtstream.WriteLine("</style>")
$txtstream.WriteLine("<title>Win32_Process</title>")
$txtstream.WriteLine("</head>")
$txtstream.WriteLine("<body>")
```

Use this if you want to create a border around your table:
```
$txtstream.WriteLine("<table Border='1' cellpadding='1' cellspacing='1'>")
```

Use this if you don't want to create a border around your table:
```
$txtstream.WriteLine("<table Border='0' cellpadding='1' cellspacing='1'>")
```

```
$txtstream.WriteLine("<%")
$obj = $objs.ItemIndex(0)
foreach($prop in $obj.Properties_)
  {
      $txtstream.WriteLine("Response.Write(""<tr><th>" + $prop.Name +
"</th>(""<td>" + GetValue($prop.Name, $obj) + "</td></tr>"" & vbcrlf)")
  }
$txtstream.WriteLine("%>")
$txtstream.WriteLine("</table>")
$txtstream.WriteLine("</body>")
$txtstream.WriteLine("</html>")
$txtstream.Close()
```

For Multi Line Vertical

```
$txtstream.WriteLine("<html>")
$txtstream.WriteLine("<head>")
$txtstream.WriteLine("<style type='text/css'>")
$txtstream.WriteLine("th")
$txtstream.WriteLine("{")
$txtstream.WriteLine("   COLOR: darkred;")
```

```
$txtstream.WriteLine("    BACKGROUND-COLOR: white;")
$txtstream.WriteLine("    FONT-FAMILY:font-family: Cambria, serif;")
$txtstream.WriteLine("    FONT-SIZE: 12px;")
$txtstream.WriteLine("    text-align: left;")
$txtstream.WriteLine("    white-Space: nowrap;")
$txtstream.WriteLine("}")
$txtstream.WriteLine("td")
$txtstream.WriteLine("{")
$txtstream.WriteLine("    COLOR: navy;")
$txtstream.WriteLine("    BACKGROUND-COLOR: white;")
$txtstream.WriteLine("    FONT-FAMILY: font-family: Cambria, serif;")
$txtstream.WriteLine("    FONT-SIZE: 12px;")
$txtstream.WriteLine("    text-align: left;")
$txtstream.WriteLine("    white-Space: nowrap;")
$txtstream.WriteLine("}")
$txtstream.WriteLine("</style>")
$txtstream.WriteLine("<title>Win32_Process</title>")
$txtstream.WriteLine("</head>")
$txtstream.WriteLine("<body>")
```

Use this if you want to create a border around your table:
```
$txtstream.WriteLine("<table Border='1' cellpadding='1' cellspacing='1'>")
```

Use this if you don't want to create a border around your table:
```
$txtstream.WriteLine("<table Border='0' cellpadding='1' cellspacing='1'>")
$txtstream.WriteLine("<%")
$obj = $objs.ItemIndex(0)
foreach($prop in $obj.Properties_)
{
    $txtstream.WriteLine("Response.Write(""<tr><th>" + $prop.Name +
"</th>"" & vbcrlf)")
    foreach($obj1 in $objs)
    {
```

```
        $txtstream.WriteLine("Response.Write(""<td>" + GetValue($prop.Name,
$obj1) + "</td>"" & vbcrlf)")
    }
    $txtstream.WriteLine("Response.Write(""</tr>"" & vbcrlf)")
}
$txtstream.WriteLine("%>")
$txtstream.WriteLine("</table>")
$txtstream.WriteLine("</body>")
$txtstream.WriteLine("</html>")
$txtstream.Close()
```

ASPX Code

B elow, is the code for ASP. The getValue function is in Appendix B.

```
$l = New-object -com WbemScripting.SWbemLocator
$svc = $l.ConnectServer(".", "root\\cimv2")
$svc.Security_.AuthenticationLevel=6")
$svc.Security_.ImpersonationLevel=3")


$ob = $svc.Get("Win32_Process")
$objs = $ob.Instances_(0)



$ws = New-object -com WScript.Shell
$txtstream = $fso.OpenTextFile($ws.CurrentDirectory +
"\Win32_Process.aspx", 2, $true, -2)
```

For Single Line Horizontal

```
$txtstream.WriteLine("<!DOCTYPE html PUBLIC ""-//W3C//DTD XHTML 1.0
Transitional//EN"" ""http://www.w3.org/TR/xhtml1/DTD/xhtml1-
transitional.dtd"">")
$txtstream.WriteLine("")
```

```
$txtstream.WriteLine("<html xmlns="http://www.w3.org/1999/xhtml"
>")
$txtstream.WriteLine("<head>")
$txtstream.WriteLine("<style type='text/css'>")
$txtstream.WriteLine("th")
$txtstream.WriteLine("{")
$txtstream.WriteLine("    COLOR: darkred;")
$txtstream.WriteLine("    BACKGROUND-COLOR: white;")
$txtstream.WriteLine("    FONT-FAMILY:font-family: Cambria, serif;")
$txtstream.WriteLine("    FONT-SIZE: 12px;")
$txtstream.WriteLine("    text-align: left;")
$txtstream.WriteLine("    white-Space: nowrap;")
$txtstream.WriteLine("}")
$txtstream.WriteLine("td")
$txtstream.WriteLine("{")
$txtstream.WriteLine("    COLOR: navy;")
$txtstream.WriteLine("    BACKGROUND-COLOR: white;")
$txtstream.WriteLine("    FONT-FAMILY: font-family: Cambria, serif;")
$txtstream.WriteLine("    FONT-SIZE: 12px;")
$txtstream.WriteLine("    text-align: left;")
$txtstream.WriteLine("    white-Space: nowrap;")
$txtstream.WriteLine("}")
$txtstream.WriteLine("</style>")
$txtstream.WriteLine("<title>Win32_Process</title>")
$txtstream.WriteLine("</head>")
$txtstream.WriteLine("<body>")
```

Use this if you want to create a border around your table:
```
$txtstream.WriteLine("<table Border='1' cellpadding='1' cellspacing='1'>")
```

Use this if you don't want to create a border around your table:
```
$txtstream.WriteLine("<table Border='0' cellpadding='1' cellspacing='1'>")
$txtstream.WriteLine("<%")
$obj = $objs.ItemIndex(0)
```

```
$txtstream.WriteLine("Response.Write(""<tr>"" & vbcrlf)")
foreach($prop in $obj.Properties_)
{
    $txtstream.WriteLine("Response.Write(""<th>" + $prop.Name + "</th>"" &
vbcrlf)")
}
$txtstream.WriteLine("Response.Write(""</tr>"" & vbcrlf)")
$txtstream.WriteLine("Response.Write(""<tr>"" & vbcrlf)")
foreach($prop in $obj.Properties_)
{
    $txtstream.WriteLine("Response.Write(""<td>" + GetValue($prop.Name,
$obj) + "</td>"" & vbcrlf)")
}
$txtstream.WriteLine("Response.Write(""</tr>"" & vbcrlf)")
$txtstream.WriteLine("%>")
$txtstream.WriteLine("</table>")
$txtstream.WriteLine("</body>")
$txtstream.WriteLine("</html>")
$txtstream.Close()
```

For Multi Line Horizontal

```
$txtstream.WriteLine("<!DOCTYPE html PUBLIC ""-//W3C//DTD XHTML 1.0
Transitional//EN"" ""http://www.w3.org/TR/xhtml1/DTD/xhtml1-
transitional.dtd"">")
$txtstream.WriteLine("")
$txtstream.WriteLine("<html xmlns="http://www.w3.org/1999/xhtml"
>")
$txtstream.WriteLine("<head>")
$txtstream.WriteLine("<style type='text/css'>")
$txtstream.WriteLine("th")
$txtstream.WriteLine("{")
$txtstream.WriteLine("    COLOR: darkred;")
$txtstream.WriteLine("    BACKGROUND-COLOR: white;")
```

```
$txtstream.WriteLine("    FONT-FAMILY:font-family: Cambria, serif;")
$txtstream.WriteLine("    FONT-SIZE: 12px;")
$txtstream.WriteLine("    text-align: left;")
$txtstream.WriteLine("    white-Space: nowrap;")
$txtstream.WriteLine("}")
$txtstream.WriteLine("td")
$txtstream.WriteLine("{")
$txtstream.WriteLine("    COLOR: navy;")
$txtstream.WriteLine("    BACKGROUND-COLOR: white;")
$txtstream.WriteLine("    FONT-FAMILY: font-family: Cambria, serif;")
$txtstream.WriteLine("    FONT-SIZE: 12px;")
$txtstream.WriteLine("    text-align: left;")
$txtstream.WriteLine("    white-Space: nowrap;")
$txtstream.WriteLine("}")
$txtstream.WriteLine("</style>")
$txtstream.WriteLine("<title>Win32_Process</title>")
$txtstream.WriteLine("</head>")
$txtstream.WriteLine("<body>")
```

Use this if you want to create a border around your table:
```
$txtstream.WriteLine("<table Border='1' cellpadding='1' cellspacing='1'>")
```

Use this if you don't want to create a border around your table:
```
$txtstream.WriteLine("<table Border='0' cellpadding='1' cellspacing='1'>")
```

```
$txtstream.WriteLine("<%")
$obj = $objs.ItemIndex(0)
$txtstream.WriteLine("Response.Write(""<tr>"" & vbcrlf)")
foreach($prop in $obj.Properties_)
{
    $txtstream.WriteLine("Response.Write(""<th>" + $prop.Name + "</th>"" &
vbcrlf)")
}
```

```
$txtstream.WriteLine("Response.Write(""</tr>"" & vbcrlf)")
foreach($obj in $objs)
{
    $txtstream.WriteLine("Response.Write(""<tr>"" & vbcrlf)")
    foreach($prop in $obj.Properties_)
    {
        $txtstream.WriteLine("Response.Write(""<td>" + GetValue($prop.Name,
$obj) + "</td>"" & vbcrlf)")
    }
    $txtstream.WriteLine("Response.Write(""</tr>"" & vbcrlf)")
}
$txtstream.WriteLine("%>")
$txtstream.WriteLine("</table>")
$txtstream.WriteLine("</body>")
$txtstream.WriteLine("</html>")
$txtstream.Close()
```

For Single Line Vertical

```
$txtstream.WriteLine("<!DOCTYPE html PUBLIC ""-//W3C//DTD XHTML 1.0
Transitional//EN"" ""http://www.w3.org/TR/xhtml1/DTD/xhtml1-
transitional.dtd"">")
$txtstream.WriteLine("")
$txtstream.WriteLine("<html xmlns="http://www.w3.org/1999/xhtml"
>")
$txtstream.WriteLine("<head>")
$txtstream.WriteLine("<style type='text/css'>")
$txtstream.WriteLine("th")
$txtstream.WriteLine("{")
$txtstream.WriteLine("   COLOR: darkred;")
$txtstream.WriteLine("   BACKGROUND-COLOR: white;")
$txtstream.WriteLine("   FONT-FAMILY:font-family: Cambria, serif;")
$txtstream.WriteLine("   FONT-SIZE: 12px;")
$txtstream.WriteLine("   text-align: left;")
$txtstream.WriteLine("   white-Space: nowrap;")
```

```
$txtstream.WriteLine("}")
$txtstream.WriteLine("td")
$txtstream.WriteLine("{")
$txtstream.WriteLine("   COLOR: navy;")
$txtstream.WriteLine("   BACKGROUND-COLOR: white;")
$txtstream.WriteLine("   FONT-FAMILY: font-family: Cambria, serif;")
$txtstream.WriteLine("   FONT-SIZE: 12px;")
$txtstream.WriteLine("   text-align: left;")
$txtstream.WriteLine("   white-Space: nowrap;")
$txtstream.WriteLine("}")
$txtstream.WriteLine("</style>")
$txtstream.WriteLine("<title>Win32_Process</title>")
$txtstream.WriteLine("</head>")
$txtstream.WriteLine("<body>")
```

Use this if you want to create a border around your table:

```
$txtstream.WriteLine("<table Border='1' cellpadding='1' cellspacing='1'>")
```

Use this if you don't want to create a border around your table:

```
$txtstream.WriteLine("<table Border='0' cellpadding='1' cellspacing='1'>")
```

```
$txtstream.WriteLine("<%")
$obj = $objs.ItemIndex(0)
foreach($prop in $obj.Properties_)
{
    $txtstream.WriteLine("Response.Write(""<tr><th>" + $prop.Name +
"</th>(""<td>" + GetValue($prop.Name, $obj) + "</td></tr>"" & vbcrlf)")
}
$txtstream.WriteLine("%>")
$txtstream.WriteLine("</table>")
$txtstream.WriteLine("</body>")
$txtstream.WriteLine("</html>")
$txtstream.Close()
```

For Multi Line Vertical

$txtstream.WriteLine("<!DOCTYPE html PUBLIC ""-//W3C//DTD XHTML 1.0 Transitional//EN"" ""http://www.w3.org/TR/xhtml1/DTD/xhtml1-transitional.dtd"">")

$txtstream.WriteLine("")

$txtstream.WriteLine("<html xmlns="http://www.w3.org/1999/xhtml" >")

$txtstream.WriteLine("<head>")

$txtstream.WriteLine("<style type='text/css'>")

$txtstream.WriteLine("th")

$txtstream.WriteLine("{")

$txtstream.WriteLine("   COLOR: darkred;")

$txtstream.WriteLine("   BACKGROUND-COLOR: white;")

$txtstream.WriteLine("   FONT-FAMILY:font-family: Cambria, serif;")

$txtstream.WriteLine("   FONT-SIZE: 12px;")

$txtstream.WriteLine("   text-align: left;")

$txtstream.WriteLine("   white-Space: nowrap;")

$txtstream.WriteLine("}")

$txtstream.WriteLine("td")

$txtstream.WriteLine("{")

$txtstream.WriteLine("   COLOR: navy;")

$txtstream.WriteLine("   BACKGROUND-COLOR: white;")

$txtstream.WriteLine("   FONT-FAMILY: font-family: Cambria, serif;")

$txtstream.WriteLine("   FONT-SIZE: 12px;")

$txtstream.WriteLine("   text-align: left;")

$txtstream.WriteLine("   white-Space: nowrap;")

$txtstream.WriteLine("}")

$txtstream.WriteLine("</style>")

$txtstream.WriteLine("<title>Win32_Process</title>")

$txtstream.WriteLine("</head>")

$txtstream.WriteLine("<body>")

Use this if you want to create a border around your table:
$txtstream.WriteLine("<table Border='1' cellpadding='1' cellspacing='1'>")

Use this if you don't want to create a border around your table:
$txtstream.WriteLine("<table Border='0' cellpadding='1' cellspacing='1'>")

```
$txtstream.WriteLine("<%")
$obj = $objs.ItemIndex(0)
foreach($prop in $obj.Properties_)
{
    $txtstream.WriteLine("Response.Write(""<tr><th>" + $prop.Name +
"</th>"" & vbcrlf)")
    foreach($obj1 in $objs)
    {
        $txtstream.WriteLine("Response.Write(""<td>" + GetValue($prop.Name,
$obj1) + "</td>"" $ vbcrlf)")
    }
    $txtstream.WriteLine("Response.Write(""</tr>"" & vbcrlf)")
}
$txtstream.WriteLine("%>")
$txtstream.WriteLine("</table")
$txtstream.WriteLine("</body>")
$txtstream.WriteLine("</html>")
$txtstream.Close()
```

HTA Code

Below, is the code for HTA. The getValue function is in Appendix B.

```
$l = New-object -com WbemScripting.SWbemLocator
$svc = $l.ConnectServer(".", "root\\cimv2")
$svc.Security_.AuthenticationLevel=6")
$svc.Security_.ImpersonationLevel=3")

$ob = $svc.Get("Win32_Process")
$objs = $ob.Instances_(0)



$ws = New-object -com WScript.Shell
$txtstream = $fso.OpenTextFile($ws.CurrentDirectory +
"\\Win32_Process.html", 2, $true, -2)
```

For Single Line Horizontal

```
$txtstream.WriteLine("<html>")
$txtstream.WriteLine("<head>")
$txtstream.WriteLine("<HTA:APPLICATION ")
```

```
$txtstream.WriteLine("ID = """Process""" ")
$txtstream.WriteLine("APPLICATIONNAME = """Process""" ")
$txtstream.WriteLine("SCROLL = """yes""" ")
$txtstream.WriteLine("SINGLEINSTANCE = """yes""" ")
$txtstream.WriteLine("WINDOWSTATE = """maximize""" >")
$txtstream.WriteLine("<style type='text/css'>")
$txtstream.WriteLine("th")
$txtstream.WriteLine("{")
$txtstream.WriteLine("    COLOR: darkred;")
$txtstream.WriteLine("    BACKGROUND-COLOR: white;")
$txtstream.WriteLine("    FONT-FAMILY:font-family: Cambria, serif;")
$txtstream.WriteLine("    FONT-SIZE: 12px;")
$txtstream.WriteLine("    text-align: left;")
$txtstream.WriteLine("    white-Space: nowrap;")
$txtstream.WriteLine("}")
$txtstream.WriteLine("td")
$txtstream.WriteLine("{")
$txtstream.WriteLine("    COLOR: navy;")
$txtstream.WriteLine("    BACKGROUND-COLOR: white;")
$txtstream.WriteLine("    FONT-FAMILY: font-family: Cambria, serif;")
$txtstream.WriteLine("    FONT-SIZE: 12px;")
$txtstream.WriteLine("    text-align: left;")
$txtstream.WriteLine("    white-Space: nowrap;")
$txtstream.WriteLine("}")
$txtstream.WriteLine("</style>")
$txtstream.WriteLine("<title>Win32_Process</title>")
$txtstream.WriteLine("</head>")
$txtstream.WriteLine("<body>")
```

Use this if you want to create a border around your table:
```
$txtstream.WriteLine("<table Border='1' cellpadding='1' cellspacing='1'>")
```

Use this if you don't want to create a border around your table:

```
$txtstream.WriteLine("<table Border='0' cellpadding='1' cellspacing='1'>")
$obj = $objs.ItemIndex(0)
$txtstream.WriteLine("<tr>")
foreach($prop in $obj.Properties_)
    $txtstream.WriteLine("<th>" + $prop.Name + "</th>)")
next
$txtstream.WriteLine("</tr>")
$txtstream.WriteLine("<tr>")
foreach($prop in $obj.Properties_)
    $txtstream.WriteLine("<td>" + GetValue($prop.Name, $obj) + "</td>)")
next
$txtstream.WriteLine("</tr>")
$txtstream.WriteLine("</table>")
$txtstream.WriteLine("</body>")
$txtstream.WriteLine("</html>")
$txtstream.Close()
```

For Multi Line Horizontal

```
$txtstream.WriteLine(html>")
$txtstream.WriteLine("<head>")
$txtstream.WriteLine("<HTA:APPLICATION ")
$txtstream.WriteLine("ID = ""Process"" ")
$txtstream.WriteLine("APPLICATIONNAME = ""Process"" ")
$txtstream.WriteLine("SCROLL = ""yes"" ")
$txtstream.WriteLine("SINGLEINSTANCE = ""yes"" ")
$txtstream.WriteLine("WINDOWSTATE = ""maximize"" >")
$txtstream.WriteLine("<style type='text/css'>")
$txtstream.WriteLine("th")
$txtstream.WriteLine("{")
$txtstream.WriteLine("    COLOR: darkred;")
$txtstream.WriteLine("    BACKGROUND-COLOR: white;")
$txtstream.WriteLine("    FONT-FAMILY:font-family: Cambria, serif;")
```

```
$txtstream.WriteLine("   FONT-SIZE: 12px;")
$txtstream.WriteLine("   text-align: left;")
$txtstream.WriteLine("   white-Space: nowrap;")
$txtstream.WriteLine("}")
$txtstream.WriteLine("td")
$txtstream.WriteLine("{")
$txtstream.WriteLine("   COLOR: navy;")
$txtstream.WriteLine("   BACKGROUND-COLOR: white;")
$txtstream.WriteLine("   FONT-FAMILY: font-family: Cambria, serif;")
$txtstream.WriteLine("   FONT-SIZE: 12px;")
$txtstream.WriteLine("   text-align: left;")
$txtstream.WriteLine("   white-Space: nowrap;")
$txtstream.WriteLine("}")
$txtstream.WriteLine("</style>")
$txtstream.WriteLine("<title>Win32_Process</title>")
$txtstream.WriteLine("</head>")
$txtstream.WriteLine("<body>")
```

Use this if you want to create a border around your table:

```
$txtstream.WriteLine("<table Border='1' cellpadding='1' cellspacing='1'>")
```

Use this if you don't want to create a border around your table:

```
$txtstream.WriteLine("<table Border='0' cellpadding='1' cellspacing='1'>")
```

```
$obj = $objs.ItemIndex(0)
$txtstream.WriteLine("<tr>")
foreach($prop in $obj.Properties_)
{
   $txtstream.WriteLine("<th>" + $prop.Name + "</th>)")
}
$txtstream.WriteLine("</tr>")
foreach($obj in $objs)
{
```

```
    $txtstream.WriteLine("<tr>")
    foreach($prop in $obj.Properties_)
    {
        $txtstream.WriteLine("<td>" + GetValue($prop.Name, $obj) + "</td>)")
    }
    $txtstream.WriteLine("</tr>")
}
$txtstream.WriteLine("</table>")
$txtstream.WriteLine("</body>")
$txtstream.WriteLine("</html>")
$txtstream.Close()
```

For Single Line Vertical

```
$txtstream.WriteLine("<html>")
$txtstream.WriteLine("<head>")
$txtstream.WriteLine("<HTA:APPLICATION ")
$txtstream.WriteLine("ID = ""Process"" ")
$txtstream.WriteLine("APPLICATIONNAME = ""Process"" ")
$txtstream.WriteLine("SCROLL = ""yes"" ")
$txtstream.WriteLine("SINGLEINSTANCE = ""yes"" ")
$txtstream.WriteLine("WINDOWSTATE = ""maximize"" >")
$txtstream.WriteLine("<style type='text/css'>")
$txtstream.WriteLine("th")
$txtstream.WriteLine("{")
$txtstream.WriteLine("    COLOR: darkred;")
$txtstream.WriteLine("    BACKGROUND-COLOR: white;")
$txtstream.WriteLine("    FONT-FAMILY:font-family: Cambria, serif;")
$txtstream.WriteLine("    FONT-SIZE: 12px;")
$txtstream.WriteLine("    text-align: left;")
$txtstream.WriteLine("    white-Space: nowrap;")
$txtstream.WriteLine("}")
```

```
$txtstream.WriteLine("td")
$txtstream.WriteLine("{")
$txtstream.WriteLine("   COLOR: navy;")
$txtstream.WriteLine("   BACKGROUND-COLOR: white;")
$txtstream.WriteLine("   FONT-FAMILY: font-family: Cambria, serif;")
$txtstream.WriteLine("   FONT-SIZE: 12px;")
$txtstream.WriteLine("   text-align: left;")
$txtstream.WriteLine("   white-Space: nowrap;")
$txtstream.WriteLine("}")
$txtstream.WriteLine("</style>")
$txtstream.WriteLine("<title>Win32_Process</title>")
$txtstream.WriteLine("</head>")
$txtstream.WriteLine("<body>")
```

Use this if you want to create a border around your table:

```
$txtstream.WriteLine("<table Border='1' cellpadding='1' cellspacing='1'>")
```

Use this if you don't want to create a border around your table:

```
$txtstream.WriteLine("<table Border='0' cellpadding='1' cellspacing='1'>")
```

```
$obj = $objs.ItemIndex(0)
foreach($prop in $obj.Properties_)
{
    $txtstream.WriteLine("<tr><th>" + $prop.Name + "</th>(""<td>" +
GetValue($prop.Name, $obj) + "</td></tr>)")
}
$txtstream.WriteLine("</table>")
$txtstream.WriteLine("</body>")
$txtstream.WriteLine("</html>")
$txtstream.Close()
```

For Multi Line Vertical

```
$txtstream.WriteLine("<html>")
```

```
$txtstream.WriteLine("<head>")
$txtstream.WriteLine("<HTA:APPLICATION ")
$txtstream.WriteLine("ID = ""Process"" ")
$txtstream.WriteLine("APPLICATIONNAME = ""Process"" ")
$txtstream.WriteLine("SCROLL = ""yes"" ")
$txtstream.WriteLine("SINGLEINSTANCE = ""yes"" ")
$txtstream.WriteLine("WINDOWSTATE = ""maximize"" >")

$txtstream.WriteLine("<style type='text/css'>")
$txtstream.WriteLine("th")
$txtstream.WriteLine("{")
$txtstream.WriteLine("   COLOR: darkred;")
$txtstream.WriteLine("   BACKGROUND-COLOR: white;")
$txtstream.WriteLine("   FONT-FAMILY:font-family: Cambria, serif;")
$txtstream.WriteLine("   FONT-SIZE: 12px;")
$txtstream.WriteLine("   text-align: left;")
$txtstream.WriteLine("   white-Space: nowrap;")
$txtstream.WriteLine("}")
$txtstream.WriteLine("td")
$txtstream.WriteLine("{")
$txtstream.WriteLine("   COLOR: navy;")
$txtstream.WriteLine("   BACKGROUND-COLOR: white;")
$txtstream.WriteLine("   FONT-FAMILY: font-family: Cambria, serif;")
$txtstream.WriteLine("   FONT-SIZE: 12px;")
$txtstream.WriteLine("   text-align: left;")
$txtstream.WriteLine("   white-Space: nowrap;")
$txtstream.WriteLine("}")
$txtstream.WriteLine("</style>")
$txtstream.WriteLine("<title>Win32_Process</title>")
$txtstream.WriteLine("</head>")
$txtstream.WriteLine("<body>")
```

Use this if you want to create a border around your table:

```
$txtstream.WriteLine("<table Border='1' cellpadding='1' cellspacing='1'>")
```

Use this if you don't want to create a border around your table:
```
$txtstream.WriteLine("<table Border='0' cellpadding='1' cellspacing='1'>")
```

```
$obj = $objs.ItemIndex(0)
foreach($prop in $obj.Properties_)
{
    $txtstream.WriteLine("<tr><th>" + $prop.Name + "</th>)")
    foreach($obj1 in $objs)
    {
        $txtstream.WriteLine("<td>" + GetValue($prop.Name, $obj1) + "</td>)")
    }
    $txtstream.WriteLine("</tr>")
}
$txtstream.WriteLine("</table>")
$txtstream.WriteLine("</body>")
$txtstream.WriteLine("</html>")
$txtstream.Close()
```

HTML Code

Below, is the code for HTML. The getValue function is in Appendix B.

```
$l = New-object -com WbemScripting.SWbemLocator
$svc = $l.ConnectServer(".", "root\\cimv2")
$svc.Security_.AuthenticationLevel=6")
$svc.Security_.ImpersonationLevel=3")

$ob = $svc.Get("Win32_Process")
$objs = $ob.Instances_(0)


$ws = New-object -com WScript.Shell
$txtstream = $fso.OpenTextFile($ws.CurrentDirectory +
"\\Win32_Process.html", 2, $true, -2)
```

For Single Line Horizontal

```
$txtstream.WriteLine("<html>")
$txtstream.WriteLine("<head>")
$txtstream.WriteLine("<style type='text/css'>")
```

```
$txtstream.WriteLine("th")
$txtstream.WriteLine("{")
$txtstream.WriteLine("    COLOR: darkred;")
$txtstream.WriteLine("    BACKGROUND-COLOR: white;")
$txtstream.WriteLine("    FONT-FAMILY:font-family: Cambria, serif;")
$txtstream.WriteLine("    FONT-SIZE: 12px;")
$txtstream.WriteLine("    text-align: left;")
$txtstream.WriteLine("    white-Space: nowrap;")
$txtstream.WriteLine("}")
$txtstream.WriteLine("td")
$txtstream.WriteLine("{")
$txtstream.WriteLine("    COLOR: navy;")
$txtstream.WriteLine("    BACKGROUND-COLOR: white;")
$txtstream.WriteLine("    FONT-FAMILY: font-family: Cambria, serif;")
$txtstream.WriteLine("    FONT-SIZE: 12px;")
$txtstream.WriteLine("    text-align: left;")
$txtstream.WriteLine("    white-Space: nowrap;")
$txtstream.WriteLine("}")
$txtstream.WriteLine("</style>")
$txtstream.WriteLine("<title>Win32_Process</title>")
$txtstream.WriteLine("</head>")
$txtstream.WriteLine("<body>")
```

Use this if you want to create a border around your table:
```
$txtstream.WriteLine("<table Border='1' cellpadding='1' cellspacing='1'>")
```

Use this if you don't want to create a border around your table:
```
$txtstream.WriteLine("<table Border='0' cellpadding='1' cellspacing='1'>")
$obj = $objs.ItemIndex(0)
$txtstream.WriteLine("<tr>")
foreach($prop in $obj.Properties_)
    $txtstream.WriteLine("<th>" + $prop.Name + "</th>)")
next
```

```
$txtstream.WriteLine("</tr>")
$txtstream.WriteLine("<tr>")
foreach($prop in $obj.Properties_)
    $txtstream.WriteLine("<td>" + GetValue($prop.Name, $obj) + "</td>)")
next
$txtstream.WriteLine("</tr>")
$txtstream.WriteLine("</table>")
$txtstream.WriteLine("</body>")
$txtstream.WriteLine("</html>")
$txtstream.Close()
```

For Multi Line Horizontal

```
$txtstream.WriteLine(html>")
$txtstream.WriteLine("<head>")
$txtstream.WriteLine("<style type='text/css'>")
$txtstream.WriteLine("th")
$txtstream.WriteLine("{")
$txtstream.WriteLine("    COLOR: darkred;")
$txtstream.WriteLine("    BACKGROUND-COLOR: white;")
$txtstream.WriteLine("    FONT-FAMILY:font-family: Cambria, serif;")
$txtstream.WriteLine("    FONT-SIZE: 12px;")
$txtstream.WriteLine("    text-align: left;")
$txtstream.WriteLine("    white-Space: nowrap;")
$txtstream.WriteLine("}")
$txtstream.WriteLine("td")
$txtstream.WriteLine("{")
$txtstream.WriteLine("    COLOR: navy;")
$txtstream.WriteLine("    BACKGROUND-COLOR: white;")
$txtstream.WriteLine("    FONT-FAMILY: font-family: Cambria, serif;")
$txtstream.WriteLine("    FONT-SIZE: 12px;")
$txtstream.WriteLine("    text-align: left;")
$txtstream.WriteLine("    white-Space: nowrap;")
```

```
$txtstream.WriteLine("}")
$txtstream.WriteLine("</style>")
$txtstream.WriteLine("<title>Win32_Process</title>")
$txtstream.WriteLine("</head>")
$txtstream.WriteLine("<body>")
```

Use this if you want to create a border around your table:

```
$txtstream.WriteLine("<table Border='1' cellpadding='1' cellspacing='1'>")
```

Use this if you don't want to create a border around your table:

```
$txtstream.WriteLine("<table Border='0' cellpadding='1' cellspacing='1'>")
```

```
$obj = $objs.ItemIndex(0)
$txtstream.WriteLine("<tr>")
foreach($prop in $obj.Properties_)
{
   $txtstream.WriteLine("<th>" + $prop.Name + "</th>)")
}
$txtstream.WriteLine("</tr>")
foreach($obj in $objs)
{
   $txtstream.WriteLine("<tr>")
   foreach($prop in $obj.Properties_)
   {
      $txtstream.WriteLine("<td>" + GetValue($prop.Name, $obj) + "</td>)")
   }
   $txtstream.WriteLine("</tr>")
}
$txtstream.WriteLine("</table>")
$txtstream.WriteLine("</body>")
$txtstream.WriteLine("</html>")
$txtstream.Close()
```

For Single Line Vertical

```
$txtstream.WriteLine("<html>")
$txtstream.WriteLine("<head>")
$txtstream.WriteLine("<style type='text/css'>")
$txtstream.WriteLine("th")
$txtstream.WriteLine("{")
$txtstream.WriteLine("   COLOR: darkred;")
$txtstream.WriteLine("   BACKGROUND-COLOR: white;")
$txtstream.WriteLine("   FONT-FAMILY:font-family: Cambria, serif;")
$txtstream.WriteLine("   FONT-SIZE: 12px;")
$txtstream.WriteLine("   text-align: left;")
$txtstream.WriteLine("   white-Space: nowrap;")
$txtstream.WriteLine("}")
$txtstream.WriteLine("td")
$txtstream.WriteLine("{")
$txtstream.WriteLine("   COLOR: navy;")
$txtstream.WriteLine("   BACKGROUND-COLOR: white;")
$txtstream.WriteLine("   FONT-FAMILY: font-family: Cambria, serif;")
$txtstream.WriteLine("   FONT-SIZE: 12px;")
$txtstream.WriteLine("   text-align: left;")
$txtstream.WriteLine("   white-Space: nowrap;")
$txtstream.WriteLine("}")
$txtstream.WriteLine("</style>")
$txtstream.WriteLine("<title>Win32_Process</title>")
$txtstream.WriteLine("</head>")
$txtstream.WriteLine("<body>")
```

Use this if you want to create a border around your table:
```
$txtstream.WriteLine("<table Border='1' cellpadding='1' cellspacing='1'>")
```

Use this if you don't want to create a border around your table:

```
$txtstream.WriteLine("<table Border='0' cellpadding='1' cellspacing='1'>")

$obj = $objs.ItemIndex(0)
foreach($prop in $obj.Properties_)
{
    $txtstream.WriteLine("<tr><th>" + $prop.Name + "</th>(""<td>" +
GetValue($prop.Name, $obj) + "</td></tr>)")
}
$txtstream.WriteLine("</table>")
$txtstream.WriteLine("</body>")
$txtstream.WriteLine("</html>")
$txtstream.Close()
```

For Multi Line Vertical

```
$txtstream.WriteLine("<html>")
$txtstream.WriteLine("<head>")
$txtstream.WriteLine("<style type='text/css'>")
$txtstream.WriteLine("th")
$txtstream.WriteLine("{")
$txtstream.WriteLine("   COLOR: darkred;")
$txtstream.WriteLine("   BACKGROUND-COLOR: white;")
$txtstream.WriteLine("   FONT-FAMILY:font-family: Cambria, serif;")
$txtstream.WriteLine("   FONT-SIZE: 12px;")
$txtstream.WriteLine("   text-align: left;")
$txtstream.WriteLine("   white-Space: nowrap;")
$txtstream.WriteLine("}")
$txtstream.WriteLine("td")
$txtstream.WriteLine("{")
$txtstream.WriteLine("   COLOR: navy;")
$txtstream.WriteLine("   BACKGROUND-COLOR: white;")
$txtstream.WriteLine("   FONT-FAMILY: font-family: Cambria, serif;")
$txtstream.WriteLine("   FONT-SIZE: 12px;")
$txtstream.WriteLine("   text-align: left;")
$txtstream.WriteLine("   white-Space: nowrap;")
```

```
$txtstream.WriteLine("}”)
$txtstream.WriteLine("</style>“)
$txtstream.WriteLine("<title>Win32_Process</title>“)
$txtstream.WriteLine("</head>“)
$txtstream.WriteLine("<body>“)
```

Use this if you want to create a border around your table:
```
$txtstream.WriteLine("<table Border='1' cellpadding='1' cellspacing='1'>“)
```

Use this if you don't want to create a border around your table:
```
$txtstream.WriteLine("<table Border='0' cellpadding='1' cellspacing='1'>“)
```

```
$obj = $objs.ItemIndex(0)
foreach($prop in $obj.Properties_)
{
   $txtstream.WriteLine("<tr><th>” + $prop.Name + "</th>)”)
   foreach($obj1 in $objs)
   {
      $txtstream.WriteLine("<td>” + GetValue($prop.Name, $obj1) + "</td>)”)
   }
   $txtstream.WriteLine(“</tr>”)
}
$txtstream.WriteLine(“</table>“)
$txtstream.WriteLine("</body>“)
$txtstream.WriteLine("</html>“)
$txtstream.Close()
```

Text Delimited File Examples

Text files can be databases, too

Below, are code samples for creating various types of delimited files. The getValue function is in Appendix B.

```
$l = New-object -com WbemScripting.SWbemLocator
$svc = $l.ConnectServer(".", "root\\cimv2")
$svc.Security_.AuthenticationLevel=6")
$svc.Security_.ImpersonationLevel=3")
$ob = $svc.Get("Win32_Process")
$objs = $ob.Instances_(0)
```

Colon Delimited

```
$tempstr = ""
$ws = New-object -com WScript.Shell
Set fso =  CreateObject("Scripting.FileSystemObject
$txtstream = $fso.OpenTextFile($ws.CurrentDirectory +
"\\Win32_Process.txt" , 2, $true, -2)
```

```
$obj = $objs.ItemIndex(0)
Foreach($prop in $obj.Properties_)
{
   if($tempstr <> "")
   {
      $tempstr = $tempstr +  "~";
   }
   $tempstr = $tempstr +  $prop.Name;
}
$txtstream.WriteLine($tempstr)
$tempstr = "";
foreach($obj in $objs)
{
   Foreach($prop in $obj.Properties_)
   {
      if($tempstr ne "")
      {
         $tempstr = $tempstr  +  "~";
      }
      $tempstr = $tempstr +  "" + GetValue($prop.Name, $obj) + "";
   }
   $txtstream.WriteLine($tempstr)
   $tempstr = "";
}
$txtstream.Close()
```

```
$obj = $objs.ItemIndex(0)
Foreach($prop in $obj.Properties_)
```

```
{
  $tempstr = $prop.Name;
  Foreach($obj in $objs)
  {
    if($tempstr ne "")
    {
    $tempstr = $tempstr + "~";
    }
    $tempstr = $tempstr + '"' + GetValue($prop.Name, $obj) + '";
  }
  $txtstream.WriteLine($tempstr)
  $tempstr = "";
}
$txtstream.Close()
```

Comma Delimited

```
$tempstr = ""
$ws = New-object -com WScript.Shell
Set fso = CreateObject("Scripting.FileSystemObject
$txtstream = $fso.OpenTextFile($ws.CurrentDirectory +
"\Win32_Process.csv" , 2, $true, -2)
```

```
$obj = $objs.ItemIndex(0)
Foreach($prop in $obj.Properties_)
{
  if($tempstr <> "")
  {
```

```
      $tempstr = $tempstr +  ",";
   }
   $tempstr = $tempstr +  $prop.Name;
}
$txtstream.WriteLine($tempstr)
$tempstr = "";
foreach($obj in $objs)
{
   Foreach($prop in $obj.Properties_)
   {
      if($tempstr ne "")
      {
         $tempstr = $tempstr  +  ",";
      }
      $tempstr = $tempstr +  "" +  GetValue($prop.Name, $obj) + "";
   }
   $txtstream.WriteLine($tempstr)
   $tempstr = "";
}
$txtstream.Close()
```

```
$obj = $objs.ItemIndex(0)
Foreach($prop in $obj.Properties_)
{
   $tempstr = $prop.Name;
   Foreach($obj in $objs)
   {
      if($tempstr ne "")
      {
      $tempstr = $tempstr  +  ",";
```

```
        }
        $tempstr = $tempstr + '"' +  GetValue($prop.Name, $obj) + '"';
      }
      $txtstream.WriteLine($tempstr)
      $tempstr = "";
    }
    $txtstream.Close()
```

Exclamation

```
    $tempstr = ""
    $ws = New-object -com WScript.Shell
    Set fso =  CreateObject("Scripting.FileSystemObject
    $txtstream = $fso.OpenTextFile($ws.CurrentDirectory +
"\\Win32_Process.txt", 2, $true, -2)
```

```
    $obj = $objs.ItemIndex(0)
    Foreach($prop in $obj.Properties_)
    {
      if($tempstr <> "")
      {
        $tempstr = $tempstr +  "!";
      }
      $tempstr = $tempstr +  $prop.Name;
    }
    $txtstream.WriteLine($tempstr)
    $tempstr = "";
    foreach($obj in $objs)
```

```
{
    Foreach($prop in $obj.Properties_)
    {
        if($tempstr ne "")
        {
            $tempstr = $tempstr  +  "!";
        }
        $tempstr = $tempstr +  "" +  GetValue($prop.Name, $obj) +  "";
    }
    $txtstream.WriteLine($tempstr)
    $tempstr = "";
}
$txtstream.Close()
```

```
$obj = $objs.ItemIndex(0)
Foreach($prop in $obj.Properties_)
{
    $tempstr = $prop.Name;
    Foreach($obj in $objs)
    {
        if($tempstr ne "")
        {
        $tempstr = $tempstr  +  "!";
        }
        $tempstr = $tempstr +  "" +  GetValue($prop.Name, $obj) +  "";
    }
    $txtstream.WriteLine($tempstr)
    $tempstr = "";
}
$txtstream.Close()
```

SEMI COLON

```
$tempstr = ""
$ws = New-object -com WScript.Shell
Set fso =  CreateObject("Scripting.FileSystemObject
$txtstream = $fso.OpenTextFile($ws.CurrentDirectory +
"\\Win32_Process.txt", 2, $true, -2)
```

HORIZONTAL

```
$obj = $objs.ItemIndex(0)
Foreach($prop in $obj.Properties_)
{
   if($tempstr <> """)
   {
      $tempstr = $tempstr +  ";";
   }
   $tempstr = $tempstr +  $prop.Name;
}
$txtstream.WriteLine($tempstr)
$tempstr = "";
foreach($obj in $objs)
{
   Foreach($prop in $obj.Properties_)
   {
      if($tempstr ne "")
      {
         $tempstr = $tempstr +  ";";
      }
```

```
    $tempstr = $tempstr + '"' + GetValue($prop.Name, $obj) + '";

  }
  $txtstream.WriteLine($tempstr)
  $tempstr = "";
}
$txtstream.Close()
```

```
$obj = $objs.ItemIndex(0)
Foreach($prop in $obj.Properties_)
{
  $tempstr = $prop.Name;
  Foreach($obj in $objs)
  {
    if($tempstr ne "")
    {
    $tempstr = $tempstr  + ";";
    }
    $tempstr = $tempstr + '"' + GetValue($prop.Name, $obj) + '";

  }
  $txtstream.WriteLine($tempstr)
  $tempstr = "";
}
$txtstream.Close()
```

Tab Delimited

```
$tempstr = ""
```

```
$ws = New-object -com WScript.Shell
Set fso =  CreateObject("Scripting.FileSystemObject
$txtstream = $fso.OpenTextFile($ws.CurrentDirectory +
"\Win32_Process.txt", 2, $true, -2)
```

```
$obj = $objs.ItemIndex(0)
Foreach($prop in $obj.Properties_)
{
   if($tempstr <> "")
   {
      $tempstr = $tempstr +  "\t";
   }
   $tempstr = $tempstr +  $prop.Name;
}
$txtstream.WriteLine($tempstr)
$tempstr = "";
foreach($obj in $objs)
{
   Foreach($prop in $obj.Properties_)
   {
      if($tempstr ne "")
      {
         $tempstr = $tempstr  + "\t";
      }
      $tempstr = $tempstr + "" + GetValue($prop.Name, $obj) + "";
   }
   $txtstream.WriteLine($tempstr)
   $tempstr = "";
}
```

```
$obj = $objs.ItemIndex(0)
Foreach($prop in $obj.Properties_)
{
   $tempstr = $prop.Name;
   Foreach($obj in $objs)
   {
      if($tempstr ne "")
      {
      $tempstr = $tempstr  +  "\t";
      }
      $tempstr = $tempstr + '"' +  GetValue($prop.Name, $obj) + '"'
   }
   $txtstream.WriteLine($tempstr)
   $tempstr = "";
}
$txtstream.Close()
```

Tilde Delimited

```
$tempstr = "";
$ws = New-object -com WScript.Shell
Set fso =  CreateObject("Scripting.FileSystemObject
$txtstream = $fso.OpenTextFile($ws.CurrentDirectory +
"\\Win32_Process.txt", 2, $true, -2)
```

69

```
$obj = $objs.ItemIndex(0)
Foreach($prop in $obj.Properties_)
{
   if($tempstr <> "")
   {
      $tempstr = $tempstr +  "~";
   }
   $tempstr = $tempstr +  $prop.Name;
}
$txtstream.WriteLine($tempstr)
$tempstr = "";
foreach($obj in $objs)
{
   Foreach($prop in $obj.Properties_)
   {
      if($tempstr ne "")
      {
         $tempstr = $tempstr  +  "~";
      }
      $tempstr = $tempstr +  "" + GetValue($prop.Name, $obj) + "";
   }
   $txtstream.WriteLine($tempstr)
   $tempstr = "";
}
$txtstream.Close()
```

```
$obj = $objs.ItemIndex(0)
Foreach($prop in $obj.Properties_)
```

```
{
    $tempstr = $prop.Name;
    Foreach($obj in $objs)
    {
        if($tempstr ne "")
        {
        $tempstr = $tempstr  +  "~";
        }
        $tempstr = $tempstr + '"' + GetValue($prop.Name, $obj) + '"';
    }
    $txtstream.WriteLine($tempstr)
    $tempstr = "";
}
$txtstream.Close()
```

THE XML FILES

Because they are out there

ELL, I THOUGHT IT WAS CATCHY. Below, are examples of different types of XML that can be used with the MSDAOSP and MSPERSIST Providers. Element XML as a standalone -no XSL referenced – can be used with the MSDAOSP Provider and Schema XML can be used with MSPersist.

Element XML

```
$l = New-object -com WbemScripting.SWbemLocator
$svc = $l.ConnectServer(".", "root\\cimv2")
$svc.Security_.AuthenticationLevel=6")
$svc.Security_.ImpersonationLevel=3")
$ob = $svc.Get("Win32_Process")
$objs = $ob.Instances_(0)

$ws = New-object -com WScript.Shell
$txtstream = $fso.OpenTextFile($ws.CurrentDirectory +
"\\Win32_Process.xml", 2, $true, -2)
$txtstream.WriteLine("<?xml version='1.0' encoding='iso-8859-1'?>")
$txtstream.WriteLine("<data>")
foreach($obj in $objs)
{
    $txtstream.WriteLine("<Win32_process>")
    foreach($prop in $obj.Properties_)
```

```
        {
            $txtstream.WriteLine("<" + $prop.Name + ">" + GetValue($prop.Name,
obj). "</" + $prop.Name + ">“)
        }
        $txtstream.WriteLine("</Win32_process>“)
    }
    $txtstream.WriteLine("</data>“)
    $txtstream.Close()
```

WMI to Element XML For XSL

```
    $l = New-object -com WbemScripting.SWbemLocator
    $svc = $l.ConnectServer(“.”, “root\\cimv2”)
    $svc.Security_.AuthenticationLevel=6”)
    $svc.Security_.ImpersonationLevel=3”)
    $ob = $svc.Get(“Win32_Process”)
    $objs = $ob.Instances_(0)

    $ws = New-object -com WScript.Shell
    $txtstream = $fso.OpenTextFile($ws.CurrentDirectory +
“\\Win32_Process.xml”, 2, $true, -2)
    $txtstream.WriteLine("<?xml version='1.0' encoding='iso-8859-1'?>“)
    $txtstream.WriteLine("<?xml-stylesheet type='Text/xsl' href=”””” +
ws.CurrentDirectory + “\\Win32_Process.xsl””?>“)

    $txtstream.WriteLine("<data>“)
    foreach($obj in $objs)
    {
        $txtstream.WriteLine("<Win32_process>“)
        foreach($prop in $obj.Properties_)
        {
```

```
      $txtstream.WriteLine("<" + $prop.Name + ">" + GetValue($prop.Name,
obj). "</" + $prop.Name + ">")
        }
      $txtstream.WriteLine("</Win32_process>")
    }
    $txtstream.WriteLine("</data>")
    $txtstream.Close()
```

SCHEMA XML

```
    $l = New-object -com WbemScripting.SWbemLocator
    $svc = $l.ConnectServer(".", "root\\cimv2")
    $svc.Security_.AuthenticationLevel=6")
    $svc.Security_.ImpersonationLevel=3")
    $ob = $svc.Get("Win32_Process")
    $objs = $ob.Instances_(0)

    $ws = New-object -com WScript.Shell
    $txtstream = $fso.OpenTextFile($ws.CurrentDirectory +
"\\Win32_Process.xml", 2, $true, -2)
    $txtstream.WriteLine("<?xml version='1.0' encoding='iso-8859-1'?>")
    $txtstream.WriteLine("<data>")
    foreach($obj in $objs)
    {
      $txtstream.WriteLine("<Win32_process>")
      foreach($prop in $obj.Properties_)
      {
        $txtstream.WriteLine("<" + $prop.Name + ">" + GetValue($prop.Name,
obj). "</" + $prop.Name + ">")
      }
      $txtstream.WriteLine("</Win32_process>")
```

```
}
$txtstream.WriteLine("</data>")
$txtstream.Close()


$rs1 = New-object -com  ("ADODB.Recordset
$rs1.ActiveConnection = "Provider=MSDAOSP; Data
Source=msxml2.DSOControl"
$rs1.Open(ws.CurrentDirectory +  "\\Win32_Process.xml")


if($fso.FileExists(ws.CurrentDirectory +  "\\Win32_Process_Schema.xml") eq
$true)
    {
      $fso.DeleteFile($ws.CurrentDirectory +  "\\Win32_Process_Schema.xml")
    }
$rs1..Save($ws.CurrentDirectory +  "\\Win32_Process_Schema.xml, 1) ;
```

EXCEL
Three ways to get the job done

T HERE ARE THREE WAYS TO PUT DATA INTO EXCEL. CREATE A COMA DELIMITED FILE AND THEN USE WS.RUN, THROUGH AUTOMATION AND BY CREATING A PHYSICAL SPREADSHEET. Below are examples of doing exactly that.

Using the comma delimited file

```
$tempstr = "";
$ws = New-object -com WScript.Shell
$fso = New-object -com  ("Scripting.FileSystemObject
$txtstream = $fso.OpenTextFile($ws.CurrentDirectory +
"\\Win32_Process.csv" , 2, $true, -2)
```

HORIZONTAL

```
$obj = $objs.ItemIndex(0)
Foreach($prop in $obj.Properties_)
{
```

```
   if($tempstr <> "“)
   {
      $tempstr = $tempstr +  ",";
   }
   $tempstr = $tempstr +  $prop.Name;
}
$txtstream.WriteLine($tempstr)
$tempstr = "”;
foreach($obj in $objs)
{
   foreach($prop in $obj.Properties_)
      if($tempstr ne "“)
      {
         $tempstr = $tempstr  +  ",";
      }
      $tempstr = $tempstr + "“ +  GetValue($prop.Name, $obj) +  "“
   }
   $txtstream.WriteLine($tempstr)
   $tempstr = "”;
}
$txtstream.Close()
$ws.Run($ws.CurrentDirectory +  "\\Win32_Process.csv”)
```

```
$obj = $objs.ItemIndex(0)
Foreach($prop in $obj.Properties_)
{
   $tempstr = $prop.Name
   Foreach($obj1 in $objs)
   {
```

```
    if($tempstr ne "")
    {
       $tempstr = $tempstr  +  ",";
    }
    $tempstr = $tempstr +  "" +  GetValue($prop.Name, $obj) +  "";
  }
  $txtstream.WriteLine($tempstr)
  $tempstr = "";
}
$txtstream.Close()


$ws.Run($ws.CurrentDirectory +  "\\Win32_Process.csv")
```

Excel Automation

```
$l = New-object -com WbemScripting.SWbemLocator
$svc = $l.ConnectServer(".", "root\\cimv2")
$svc.Security_.AuthenticationLevel=6")
$svc.Security_.ImpersonationLevel=3")
$ob = $svc.Get("Win32_Process")
$objs = $ob.Instances_(0)


$oExcel = New-object -com  ("Excel.Application
$oExcel.Visible = $true;
$wb = $oExcel.Workbooks.Add()
$ws = $wb.Worksheets(0)
$ws.Name = "Win32_Process";
```

```
$y=2;
$x=1;
$obj = $objs.ItemIndex(0)
foreach($prop in $obj.Properties_)
{
    $ws.Cells.Item(1, $x) = $prop.Name;
    $x=$x. 1;
}
$x=1;
foreach($obj in $objs)
{
    foreach($prop in $obj.Properties_))
    {
        $ws.Cells.Item($y, $x) = GetValue($prop.Name, obj)
        $x=$x. 1;
    }
    $x=1;
    $y=$y. 1;
}
$ws.Columns.HorizontalAlignment = -4131;
$ws.Columns.AutoFit()
```

FOR A VERTICAL VIEW

```
$l = New-object -com WbemScripting.SWbemLocator
$svc = $l.ConnectServer(".", "root\\cimv2")
$svc.Security_.AuthenticationLevel=6")
$svc.Security_.ImpersonationLevel=3")
$ob = $svc.Get("Win32_Process")
$objs = $ob.Instances_(0)
```

```
$oExcel = New-object -com  ("Excel.Application
$oExcel.Visible = $true;
$wb = $oExcel.Workbooks.Add()
$ws = $wb.Worksheets(0)
$ws.Name = "Win32_Process";
$y=2;
$x=1;
$obj = $objs.ItemIndex(0)
foreach($prop in $obj.Properties_)
{
   $ws.Cells.Item($x, 1) = $prop.Name;
   $x=$x. 1;
}
$x=1;
foreach($obj in $objs)
{
   foreach($prop in $obj.Properties_))
   {
      $ws.Cells.Item($x, $y) = GetValue($prop.Name, obj)
      $x=$x. 1;
   }
   $x=1;
   $y=$y. 1;
}
$ws.Columns.HorizontalAlignment = -4131;
$ws.Columns.AutoFit()
```

Using A Spreadsheet

```
$l = New-object -com WbemScripting.SWbemLocator
$svc = $l.ConnectServer(".", "root\\cimv2")
```

```
$svc.Security_.AuthenticationLevel=6")
$svc.Security_.ImpersonationLevel=3")
$ob = $svc.Get("Win32_Process")
$objs = $ob.Instances_(0)
```

```
$ws = New-object -com WScript.Shell
$fso = New-object -com Scripting.FileSystemObject
$txtstream = $fso.OpenTextFile($ws.CurrentDirectory + "\\ProcessExcel.xml",
2, $true, -2)
$txtstream.WriteLine("<?xml version='1.0'?>")
$txtstream.WriteLine("<?mso-application progid='Excel.Sheet'?>")
$txtstream.WriteLine("<Workbook xmlns='urn:schemas-microsoft-
com:office:spreadsheet' xmlns:o='urn:schemas-microsoft-com:office:office'
xmlns:x='urn:schemas-microsoft-com:office:excel' xmlns:ss='urn:schemas-
microsoft-com:office:spreadsheet' xmlns:html='http://www.w3.org/TR/REC-
html40'>")
$txtstream.WriteLine("          <Document$properties xmlns='urn:schemas-
microsoft-com:office:office'>")
$txtstream.WriteLine("                    <Author>Windows User</Author>")
$txtstream.WriteLine("                    <LastAuthor>Windows
User</LastAuthor>")
$txtstream.WriteLine("                    <Created>2007-11-
27T19:36:16Z</Created>")
$txtstream.WriteLine("                    <Version>12.00</Version>")
$txtstream.WriteLine("          </Document$properties>")
$txtstream.WriteLine("          <ExcelWorkbook xmlns='urn:schemas-
microsoft-com:office:excel'>")
$txtstream.WriteLine("
     <WindowHeight>11835</WindowHeight>")
```

```
$txtstream.WriteLine("
    <WindowWidth>18960</WindowWidth>")
$txtstream.WriteLine("                    <WindowTopX>120</WindowTopX>")
$txtstream.WriteLine("                    <WindowTopY>135</WindowTopY>")
$txtstream.WriteLine("
    <ProtectStructure>False</ProtectStructure>")
$txtstream.WriteLine("
    <ProtectWindows>False</ProtectWindows>")
$txtstream.WriteLine("       </ExcelWorkbook>")
$txtstream.WriteLine("      <Styles>")
$txtstream.WriteLine("              <Style ss:ID='Default'
ss:Name='Normal'>")
$txtstream.WriteLine("                    <Alignment
ss:Vertical='Bottom'/>")
$txtstream.WriteLine("                    <Borders/>")
$txtstream.WriteLine("                    <Font ss:FontName='Calibri'
x:Family='Swiss' ss:Size='11' ss:Color='#000000'/>")
$txtstream.WriteLine("                    <Interior/>")
$txtstream.WriteLine("                    <NumberFormat/>")
$txtstream.WriteLine("                    <Protection/>")
$txtstream.WriteLine("             </Style>")
$txtstream.WriteLine("            <Style ss:ID='s62'>")
$txtstream.WriteLine("                    <Borders/>")
$txtstream.WriteLine("                    <Font ss:FontName='Calibri'
x:Family='Swiss' ss:Size='11' ss:Color='#000000' ss:Bold='1'/>")
$txtstream.WriteLine("             </Style>")
$txtstream.WriteLine("            <Style ss:ID='s63'>")
$txtstream.WriteLine("                    <Alignment
ss:Horizontal='Left' ss:Vertical='Bottom' ss:Indent='2'/>")
$txtstream.WriteLine("                    <Font ss:FontName='Verdana'
x:Family='Swiss' ss:Size='7.7' ss:Color='#000000'/>")
$txtstream.WriteLine("             </Style>")
$txtstream.WriteLine("   </Styles>")
```

```
$txtstream.WriteLine("<Worksheet ss:Name='Process'>")
$txtstream.WriteLine("  <Table x:FullColumns='1' x:FullRows='1'
ss:DefaultRowHeight='24.9375'>")
$txtstream.WriteLine("    <Column ss:AutoFitWidth='1' ss:Width='82.5'
ss:Span='5'/>")
Foreach($obj in $objs)
{
    $txtstream.WriteLine("    <Row ss:AutoFitHeight='0'>")
    Foreach($prop in $obj.Properties_)
    {
        $txtstream.WriteLine("      <Cell ss:StyleID='s62'><Data
ss:Type='String'>" + $prop.Name + "</Data></Cell>")
    }
    $txtstream.WriteLine("    </Row>")
    Break
}


Foreach($obj in $objs)
{
    $txtstream.WriteLine("    <Row ss:AutoFitHeight='0' ss:Height='13.5'>")
    foreach($prop in $obj.Properties_)
    {
        $txtstream.WriteLine("      <Cell><Data ss:Type='String'><![CDATA[" +
GetValue($prop.Name, $obj) + "]]></Data></Cell>")
    }
    $txtstream.WriteLine("    </Row>")
}
$txtstream.WriteLine("  </Table>")
$txtstream.WriteLine("    <WorksheetOptions xmlns='urn:schemas-
microsoft-com:office:excel'>")
$txtstream.WriteLine("        <PageSetup>")
$txtstream.WriteLine("          <Header x:Margin='0.3'/>")
```

```
$txtstream.WriteLine("                              <Footer x:Margin='0.3'/>")
$txtstream.WriteLine("                              <PageMargins x:Bottom='0.75'
x:Left='0.7' x:Right='0.7' x:Top='0.75'/>")
$txtstream.WriteLine("                </PageSetup>")
$txtstream.WriteLine("                <Unsynced/>")
$txtstream.WriteLine("                <Print>")
$txtstream.WriteLine("                    <FitHeight>0</FitHeight>")
$txtstream.WriteLine("                    <ValidPrinterInfo/>")
$txtstream.WriteLine("
    <HorizontalResolution>600</HorizontalResolution>")
$txtstream.WriteLine("
    <VerticalResolution>600</VerticalResolution>")
$txtstream.WriteLine("                </Print>")
$txtstream.WriteLine("                <Selected/>")
$txtstream.WriteLine("                <Panes>")
$txtstream.WriteLine("                    <Pane>")
$txtstream.WriteLine("
    <Number>3</Number>")
$txtstream.WriteLine("
    <ActiveRow>9</ActiveRow>")
$txtstream.WriteLine("
    <ActiveCol>7</ActiveCol>")
$txtstream.WriteLine("                    </Pane>")
$txtstream.WriteLine("                </Panes>")
$txtstream.WriteLine("
    <ProtectObjects>False</ProtectObjects>")
$txtstream.WriteLine("
    <ProtectScenarios>False</ProtectScenarios>")
$txtstream.WriteLine("        </WorksheetOptions>")
$txtstream.WriteLine("</Worksheet>")
$txtstream.WriteLine("</Workbook>")
$txtstream.Close()()
ws.Run(ws.CurrentDirectory +  "\ProcessExcel.xml")
```

XSL

The end of the line

B ELOW ARE WAYS YOU CAN CREATE XSL FILES TO RENDER YOU XML. Viewer discretion is advised.

```
$l = New-object -com WbemScripting.SWbemLocator
$svc = $l.ConnectServer(".", "root\\cimv2")
$svc.Security_.AuthenticationLevel=6")
$svc.Security_.ImpersonationLevel=3")
$ob = $svc.Get("Win32_Process")
$objs = $ob.Instances_(0)


$ws = New-object -com WScript.Shell
$fso = New-object -com Scripting.FileSystemObject
$txtstream= $fso.OpenTextFile($ws.CurrentDirectory + "\\Process.xsl", 2,
$true, -2)
```

SINGLE LINE HORIZONTAL

```
$txtstream.WriteLine("<?xml version=““1.0” " encoding=““UTF-8” "?>“)
$txtstream.WriteLine("<xsl:stylesheet version=““1.0”"
xmlns:xsl=““http://www.w3.org/1999/XSL/Transform” ">“)
$txtstream.WriteLine("<xsl:template match=““/”“>“)
$txtstream.WriteLine("<html>“)
$txtstream.WriteLine("<head>“)
$txtstream.WriteLine("<title>Products</title>“)
$txtstream.WriteLine("<style type='text/css'>“)
$txtstream.WriteLine("th”)
$txtstream.WriteLine("{“)
$txtstream.WriteLine("    COLOR: darkred;”)
$txtstream.WriteLine("    BACKGROUND-COLOR: white;”)
$txtstream.WriteLine("    FONT-FAMILY:font-family: Cambria, serif;”)
$txtstream.WriteLine("    FONT-SIZE: 12px;”)
$txtstream.WriteLine("    text-align: left;”)
$txtstream.WriteLine("    white-Space: nowrap;”)
$txtstream.WriteLine("}”)
$txtstream.WriteLine("td”)
$txtstream.WriteLine("{“)
$txtstream.WriteLine("    COLOR: navy;”)
$txtstream.WriteLine("    BACKGROUND-COLOR: white;”)
$txtstream.WriteLine("    FONT-FAMILY: font-family: Cambria, serif;”)
$txtstream.WriteLine("    FONT-SIZE: 12px;”)
$txtstream.WriteLine("    text-align: left;”)
$txtstream.WriteLine("    white-Space: nowrap;”)
$txtstream.WriteLine("}”)
```

```
$txtstream.WriteLine("</style>")
$txtstream.WriteLine("</head>")
$txtstream.WriteLine("<body bgcolor=""#333333" ">")
$txtstream.WriteLine("<table colspacing=""3" " colpadding=""3" ">")
$obj = $objs.ItemIndex(0)
$txtstream.WriteLine("<tr>")
foreach($prop in $obj.Properties_)
{
    $txtstream.WriteLine("<th>" + $prop.Name + </th>")
}
$txtstream.WriteLine("</tr>")
$txtstream.WriteLine("<tr>")
foreach($prop in $obj.Properties_)
{
    $txtstream.WriteLine("<td><xsl:value-of select=""data/Win32_Process/" +
$prop.Name + """/></td>")
}
$txtstream.WriteLine("</tr>")
$txtstream.WriteLine("</table>")
$txtstream.WriteLine("</body>")
$txtstream.WriteLine("</html>")
$txtstream.WriteLine("</xsl:template>")
$txtstream.WriteLine("</xsl:stylesheet>")
$txtstream.Close()()
```

For Multi Line Horizontal

```
$txtstream.WriteLine("<?xml version=""1.0" " encoding=""UTF-8" "?>")
$txtstream.WriteLine("<xsl:stylesheet version=""1.0""
xmlns:xsl=""http://www.w3.org/1999/XSL/Transform" ">")
$txtstream.WriteLine("<xsl:template match=""/"">")
```

```
$txtstream.WriteLine("<html>")
$txtstream.WriteLine("<head>")
$txtstream.WriteLine("<title>Products</title>")
$txtstream.WriteLine("<style type='text/css'>")
$txtstream.WriteLine("th")
$txtstream.WriteLine("{")
$txtstream.WriteLine("    COLOR: darkred;")
$txtstream.WriteLine("    BACKGROUND-COLOR: white;")
$txtstream.WriteLine("    FONT-FAMILY:font-family: Cambria, serif;")
$txtstream.WriteLine("    FONT-SIZE: 12px;")
$txtstream.WriteLine("   text-align: left;")
$txtstream.WriteLine("   white-Space: nowrap;")
$txtstream.WriteLine("}")
$txtstream.WriteLine("td")
$txtstream.WriteLine("{")
$txtstream.WriteLine("    COLOR: navy;")
$txtstream.WriteLine("    BACKGROUND-COLOR: white;")
$txtstream.WriteLine("    FONT-FAMILY: font-family: Cambria, serif;")
$txtstream.WriteLine("    FONT-SIZE: 12px;")
$txtstream.WriteLine("   text-align: left;")
$txtstream.WriteLine("   white-Space: nowrap;")
$txtstream.WriteLine("}")
$txtstream.WriteLine("</style>")
$txtstream.WriteLine("</head>")
$txtstream.WriteLine("<body bgcolor=""#333333" ">")
$txtstream.WriteLine("<table colspacing=""3" " colpadding=""3" ">")


$obj = $objs.ItemIndex(0)
$txtstream.WriteLine("<tr>")
foreach($prop in $obj.Properties_)
{
   $txtstream.WriteLine("<th>" + $prop.Name +  </th>")
```

```
        }
        $txtstream.WriteLine("</tr>")
        $txtstream.WriteLine("<xsl:for-each select=""data/Win32_Process"">")
        $txtstream.WriteLine("<tr>")
        foreach($prop in $obj.Properties_)
        {
            $txtstream.WriteLine("<td><xsl:value-of select="" + $prop.Name +
"""/></td>")
        }
        $txtstream.WriteLine("</tr>")
        $txtstream.WriteLine("</xsl:for-each>")
        $txtstream.WriteLine("</table>")
        $txtstream.WriteLine("</body>")
        $txtstream.WriteLine("</html>")
        $txtstream.WriteLine("</xsl:template>")
        $txtstream.WriteLine("</xsl:stylesheet>")
        $txtstream.Close()()
```

For Single Line Vertical

```
        $txtstream.WriteLine("<?xml version=""1.0" " encoding=""UTF-8" "?>")
        $txtstream.WriteLine("<xsl:stylesheet version=""1.0""
xmlns:xsl=""http://www.w3.org/1999/XSL/Transform" ">")
        $txtstream.WriteLine("<xsl:template match=""/"">")
        $txtstream.WriteLine("<html>")
        $txtstream.WriteLine("<head>")
        $txtstream.WriteLine("<title>Products</title>")
        $txtstream.WriteLine("<style type='text/css'>")
        $txtstream.WriteLine("th")
        $txtstream.WriteLine("{")
        $txtstream.WriteLine("    COLOR: darkred;")
        $txtstream.WriteLine("    BACKGROUND-COLOR: white;")
```

```
$txtstream.WriteLine("    FONT-FAMILY:font-family: Cambria, serif;")
$txtstream.WriteLine("    FONT-SIZE: 12px;")
$txtstream.WriteLine("    text-align: left;")
$txtstream.WriteLine("    white-Space: nowrap;")
$txtstream.WriteLine("}")
$txtstream.WriteLine("td")
$txtstream.WriteLine("{")
$txtstream.WriteLine("    COLOR: navy;")
$txtstream.WriteLine("    BACKGROUND-COLOR: white;")
$txtstream.WriteLine("    FONT-FAMILY: font-family: Cambria, serif;")
$txtstream.WriteLine("    FONT-SIZE: 12px;")
$txtstream.WriteLine("    text-align: left;")
$txtstream.WriteLine("    white-Space: nowrap;")
$txtstream.WriteLine("}")
$txtstream.WriteLine("</style>")
$txtstream.WriteLine("</head>")
$txtstream.WriteLine("<body bgcolor=""#333333" ">")
$txtstream.WriteLine("<table colspacing=""3" " colpadding=""3" ">")

obj = objs.ItemIndex[0]
foreach($prop in $obj.Properties_)
{
    $txtstream.WriteLine("<tr><th>" + $prop.Name + </th>")
    $txtstream.WriteLine("<td><xsl:value-of select="""data/Win32_Process/" +
$prop.Name + """/></td></tr>")
}
$txtstream.WriteLine("</table>")
$txtstream.WriteLine("</body>")
$txtstream.WriteLine("</html>")
$txtstream.WriteLine("</xsl:template>")
$txtstream.WriteLine("</xsl:stylesheet>")
$txtstream.Close()()
```

For Multi Line Vertical

```
$txtstream.WriteLine("<?xml version=""1.0" " encoding=""UTF-8" "?>")
$txtstream.WriteLine("<xsl:stylesheet version=""1.0""
xmlns:xsl=""http://www.w3.org/1999/XSL/Transform" ">")
$txtstream.WriteLine("<xsl:template match=""/"">")
$txtstream.WriteLine("<html>")
$txtstream.WriteLine("<head>")
$txtstream.WriteLine("<title>Products</title>")
$txtstream.WriteLine("<style type='text/css'>")
$txtstream.WriteLine("th")
$txtstream.WriteLine("{")
$txtstream.WriteLine("   COLOR: darkred;")
$txtstream.WriteLine("   BACKGROUND-COLOR: white;")
$txtstream.WriteLine("   FONT-FAMILY:font-family: Cambria, serif;")
$txtstream.WriteLine("   FONT-SIZE: 12px;")
$txtstream.WriteLine("   text-align: left;")
$txtstream.WriteLine("   white-Space: nowrap;")
$txtstream.WriteLine("}")
$txtstream.WriteLine("td")
$txtstream.WriteLine("{")
$txtstream.WriteLine("   COLOR: navy;")
$txtstream.WriteLine("   BACKGROUND-COLOR: white;")
$txtstream.WriteLine("   FONT-FAMILY: font-family: Cambria, serif;")
$txtstream.WriteLine("   FONT-SIZE: 12px;")
$txtstream.WriteLine("   text-align: left;")
$txtstream.WriteLine("   white-Space: nowrap;")
```

```
$txtstream.WriteLine("}")
$txtstream.WriteLine("</style>")
$txtstream.WriteLine("</head>")
$txtstream.WriteLine("<body bgcolor=""#333333" ">")
$txtstream.WriteLine("<table colspacing=""3" " colpadding=""3" ">")

$txtstream.WriteLine("<tr>")
obj = objs.ItemIndex[0]
foreach($prop in $obj.Properties_)
    $txtstream.WriteLine("<tr><th>" + $prop.Name + </th>")
    $txtstream.WriteLine("<td><xsl:for-each
select=""data/Win32_Process"">")
    $txtstream.WriteLine("<xsl:value-of select=""" + $prop.Name +
"""/></td>")
    $txtstream.WriteLine("</xsl:for-each></tr>")
next
$txtstream.WriteLine("</table>")
$txtstream.WriteLine("</body>")
$txtstream.WriteLine("</html>")
$txtstream.WriteLine("</xsl:template>")
$txtstream.WriteLine("</xsl:stylesheet>")
$txtstream.Close()()
```

Stylesheets

The difference between boring and oh, wow!

T
HE FIRST PARAGRAPH STYLE GIVES you nice spacing after the
title, as well as the right indents for the first part of your text. Try adding
uppercase letters to half of the first line for added styling. For even more
stylistic impact, add a

Style sheets:

The stylesheets in Appendix A, were used to render these pages. If you find one you like, feel free to use it.

Report:

Table

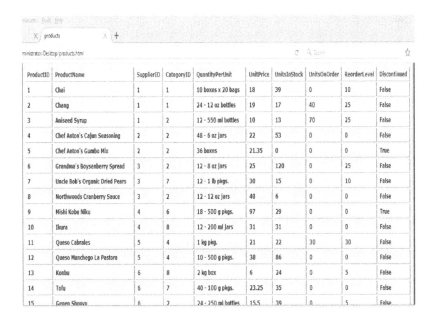

None:

Black and White

Colored:

AccountExpires	AuthorizationFlags	BadPasswordCount	Caption	CodePage	Comment	CountryCode	Description
			NT AUTHORITY\SYSTEM				Network login profile settings for SYSTEM on NT AUTHORITY
			NT AUTHORITY\LOCAL SERVICE				Network login profile settings for LOCAL SERVICE on NT AUTHORITY
			NT AUTHORITY\NETWORK SERVICE				Network login profile settings for NETWORK SERVICE on NT AUTHORITY
	0	0	Administrator	0	Built-in account for administering the computer/domain	0	Network login profile settings for on WIN-8JRLOAKMF3B
			NT SERVICE\SSASTELEMETRY				Network login profile settings for SSASTELEMETRY on NT SERVICE
			NT SERVICE\SQLTELEMETRY130				Network login profile settings for SQLTELEMETRY130 on NT SERVICE
			NT SERVICE\SQLTELEMETRY				Network login profile settings for SQLTELEMETRY on NT SERVICE
			NT SERVICE\MSSQLServerOLAPService				Network login profile settings for MSSQLServerOLAPService on NT SERVICE
			NT SERVICE\ReportServer				Network login profile settings for ReportServer on NT SERVICE
			NT SERVICE\MSSQLFDLauncher				Network login profile settings for MSSQLFDLauncher on NT SERVICE
			NT SERVICE\MSSQLLaunchpad				Network login profile settings for MSSQLLaunchpad on NT SERVICE
			NT SERVICE\MsDtsServer130				Network login profile settings for MsDtsServer130 on NT SERVICE
			NT SERVICE\MSSQLSERVER				Network login profile settings for MSSQLSERVER on NT SERVICE
			IIS APPPOOL\Classic .NET AppPool				Network login profile settings for Classic .NET AppPool on IIS APPPOOL
			IIS APPPOOL\.NET v4.5				Network login profile settings for .NET v4.5 on IIS APPPOOL
			IIS APPPOOL\.NET v2.0				Network login profile settings for .NET v2.0 on IIS APPPOOL
			IIS APPPOOL\.NET v4.5 Classic				Network login profile settings for .NET v4.5 Classic on IIS APPPOOL
			IIS APPPOOL\.NET v2.0 Classic				Network login profile settings for .NET v2.0 Classic on IIS APPPOOL

Oscillating:

Availability	BytesPerSector	Capabilities	CapabilityDescriptions	Caption	CompressionMethod	ConfigManagerErrorCode	ConfigManagerUserConfig
512	3, 4, 10	Random Access, Supports Writing, SMART Notification	OCZ REVODRIVE350 SCSI Disk Device		0	FALSE
512	3, 4	Random Access, Supports Writing	NVMe TOSHIBA-RD400		0	FALSE
512	3, 4, 10	Random Access, Supports Writing, SMART Notification	TOSHIBA DT01ACA200		0	FALSE

3D:

Availability	BytesPerSector	Capabilities	CapabilityDescriptions	Caption	CompressionMethod	ConfigManagerErrorCode	ConfigManagerUserConfig	CreationClassName
	512	3, 4, 10	Random Access, Supports Writing, SMART Notification	OCZ REVODRIVE350 SCSI Disk Device		0	FALSE	Win32_DiskDrive
	512	3, 4	Random Access, Supports Writing	NVMe TOSHIBA-RD400		0	FALSE	Win32_DiskDrive
	512	3, 4, 10	Random Access, Supports Writing, SMART Notification	TOSHIBA DT01ACA200		0	FALSE	Win32_DiskDrive

Shadow Box:

Availability	BytesPerSector	Capabilities	CapabilityDescriptions	Caption	CompressionMethod	ConfigManagerErrorCode	ConfigManagerUserConfig	CreationClassName	DefaultBlockSize
	512	3, 4, 10	Random Access, Supports Writing, SMART Notification	OCZ REVODRIVE350 SCSI Disk Device		0	FALSE	Win32_DiskDrive	
	512	3, 4	Random Access, Supports Writing	NVMe TOSHIBA-RD400		0	FALSE	Win32_DiskDrive	
	512	3, 4, 10	Random Access, Supports Writing, SMART Notification	TOSHIBA DT01ACA200		0	FALSE	Win32_DiskDrive	

Shadow Box Single Line Vertical

BiosCharacteristics	7, 10, 11, 12, 15, 16, 17, 19, 23, 24, 25, 26, 27, 28, 29, 32, 33, 40, 42, 43, 48, 50, 58, 59, 64, 65, 66, 67, 68, 69, 70, 71, 72, 73, 74, 75, 76, 77, 78, 79
BIOSVersion	ALASKA - 1072009, 0504, American Megatrends - 5000C
BuildNumber	
Caption	0504
CodeSet	
CurrentLanguage	en|US|iso8859-1
Description	0504
IdentificationCode	
InstallableLanguages	8
InstallDate	
LanguageEdition	
ListOfLanguages	en|US|iso8859-1, fr|FR|iso8859-1, zh|CN|unicode, , , , ,
Manufacturer	American Megatrends Inc.
Name	0504
OtherTargetOS	
PrimaryBIOS	TRUE

Shadow Box Multi line Vertical

Availability			
BytesPerSector	512	512	512
Capabilities	3, 4, 10	3, 4	3, 4, 10
CapabilityDescriptions	Random Access, Supports Writing, SMART Notification	Random Access, Supports Writing	Random Access, Supports Writing, SMART Notification
Caption	OCZ-REVODRIVE350 SCSI Disk Device	NVMe TOSHIBA-RD400	TOSHIBA DT01ACA200
CompressionMethod			
ConfigManagerErrorCode	0	0	0
ConfigManagerUserConfig	FALSE	FALSE	FALSE
CreationClassName	Win32_DiskDrive	Win32_DiskDrive	Win32_DiskDrive
DefaultBlockSize			
Description	Disk drive	Disk drive	Disk drive
DeviceID	\\.\PHYSICALDRIVE2	\\.\PHYSICALDRIVE1	\\.\PHYSICALDRIVE0
ErrorCleared			
ErrorDescription			
ErrorMethodology			
FirmwareRevision	2.10	57CA4102	MX4OABB0
Index	2	1	0

Stylesheets

Decorating your web pages

B ELOW ARE SOME STYLESHEETS I COOKED UP THAT I LIKE AND THINK YOU MIGHT TOO. Don't worry I won't be offended if you take and modify to your hearts delight. Please do!

NONE

```
$txtstream.WriteLine("<style type='text/css'>")
$txtstream.WriteLine("th")
$txtstream.WriteLine("{")
$txtstream.WriteLine("   COLOR: white;")
$txtstream.WriteLine("}")
$txtstream.WriteLine("td")
$txtstream.WriteLine("{")
$txtstream.WriteLine("   COLOR: white;")
$txtstream.WriteLine("}")
$txtstream.WriteLine("</style>")
```

```
$txtstream.WriteLine("<style type='text/css'>")
$txtstream.WriteLine("th")
$txtstream.WriteLine("{")
$txtstream.WriteLine("   COLOR: white;")
$txtstream.WriteLine("   BACKGROUND-COLOR: black;")
$txtstream.WriteLine("   FONT-FAMILY:font-family: Cambria, serif;")
$txtstream.WriteLine("   FONT-SIZE: 12px;")
$txtstream.WriteLine("   text-align: left;")
$txtstream.WriteLine("   white-Space: nowrap;")
$txtstream.WriteLine("}")
$txtstream.WriteLine("td")
$txtstream.WriteLine("{")
$txtstream.WriteLine("   COLOR: white;")
$txtstream.WriteLine("   BACKGROUND-COLOR: black;")
$txtstream.WriteLine("   FONT-FAMILY: font-family: Cambria, serif;")
$txtstream.WriteLine("   FONT-SIZE: 12px;")
$txtstream.WriteLine("   text-align: left;")
$txtstream.WriteLine("   white-Space: nowrap;")
$txtstream.WriteLine("}")
$txtstream.WriteLine("div")
$txtstream.WriteLine("{")
$txtstream.WriteLine("   COLOR: white;")
$txtstream.WriteLine("   BACKGROUND-COLOR: black;")
$txtstream.WriteLine("   FONT-FAMILY: font-family: Cambria, serif;")
$txtstream.WriteLine("   FONT-SIZE: 10px;")
$txtstream.WriteLine("   text-align: left;")
$txtstream.WriteLine("   white-Space: nowrap;")
$txtstream.WriteLine("}")
$txtstream.WriteLine("span")
$txtstream.WriteLine("{")
$txtstream.WriteLine("   COLOR: white;")
```

```
$txtstream.WriteLine("   BACKGROUND-COLOR: black;")
$txtstream.WriteLine("   FONT-FAMILY: font-family: Cambria, serif;")
$txtstream.WriteLine("   FONT-SIZE: 10px;")
$txtstream.WriteLine("   text-align: left;")
$txtstream.WriteLine("   white-Space: nowrap;")
$txtstream.WriteLine("   display:inline-block;")
$txtstream.WriteLine("   width: 100%;")
$txtstream.WriteLine("}")
$txtstream.WriteLine("textarea")
$txtstream.WriteLine("{")
$txtstream.WriteLine("   COLOR: white;")
$txtstream.WriteLine("   BACKGROUND-COLOR: black;")
$txtstream.WriteLine("   FONT-FAMILY: font-family: Cambria, serif;")
$txtstream.WriteLine("   FONT-SIZE: 10px;")
$txtstream.WriteLine("   text-align: left;")
$txtstream.WriteLine("   white-Space: nowrap;")
$txtstream.WriteLine("   width: 100%;")
$txtstream.WriteLine("}")
$txtstream.WriteLine("select")
$txtstream.WriteLine("{")
$txtstream.WriteLine("   COLOR: white;")
$txtstream.WriteLine("   BACKGROUND-COLOR: black;")
$txtstream.WriteLine("   FONT-FAMILY: font-family: Cambria, serif;")
$txtstream.WriteLine("   FONT-SIZE: 10px;")
$txtstream.WriteLine("   text-align: left;")
$txtstream.WriteLine("   white-Space: nowrap;")
$txtstream.WriteLine("   width: 100%;")
$txtstream.WriteLine("}")
$txtstream.WriteLine("input")
$txtstream.WriteLine("{")
$txtstream.WriteLine("   COLOR: white;")
$txtstream.WriteLine("   BACKGROUND-COLOR: black;")
$txtstream.WriteLine("   FONT-FAMILY: font-family: Cambria, serif;")
```

```
$txtstream.WriteLine("   FONT-SIZE: 12px;")
$txtstream.WriteLine("   text-align: left;")
$txtstream.WriteLine("   display:table-cell;")
$txtstream.WriteLine("   white-Space: nowrap;")
$txtstream.WriteLine("}")
$txtstream.WriteLine("h1 {")
$txtstream.WriteLine("color: antiquewhite;")
$txtstream.WriteLine("text-shadow: 1px 1px 1px black;")
$txtstream.WriteLine("padding: 3px;")
$txtstream.WriteLine("text-align: center;")
$txtstream.WriteLine("box-shadow: inset 2px 2px 5px rgba(0,0,0,0.5), inset -
2px -2px 5px rgba(255,255,255,0.5)")
$txtstream.WriteLine("}")
$txtstream.WriteLine("</style>")
```

COLORED TEXT

```
$txtstream.WriteLine("<style type='text/css'>")
$txtstream.WriteLine("th")
$txtstream.WriteLine("{")
$txtstream.WriteLine("   COLOR: darkred;")
$txtstream.WriteLine("   BACKGROUND-COLOR: #eeeeee;")
$txtstream.WriteLine("   FONT-FAMILY:font-family: Cambria, serif;")
$txtstream.WriteLine("   FONT-SIZE: 12px;")
$txtstream.WriteLine("   text-align: left;")
$txtstream.WriteLine("   white-Space: nowrap;")
$txtstream.WriteLine("}")
$txtstream.WriteLine("td")
$txtstream.WriteLine("{")
$txtstream.WriteLine("   COLOR: navy;")
$txtstream.WriteLine("   BACKGROUND-COLOR: #eeeeee;")
$txtstream.WriteLine("   FONT-FAMILY: font-family: Cambria, serif;")
$txtstream.WriteLine("   FONT-SIZE: 12px;")
```

```
$txtstream.WriteLine("   text-align: left;")
$txtstream.WriteLine("   white-Space: nowrap;")
$txtstream.WriteLine("}")
$txtstream.WriteLine("div")
$txtstream.WriteLine("{")
$txtstream.WriteLine("   COLOR: white;")
$txtstream.WriteLine("   BACKGROUND-COLOR: navy;")
$txtstream.WriteLine("   FONT-FAMILY: font-family: Cambria, serif;")
$txtstream.WriteLine("   FONT-SIZE: 10px;")
$txtstream.WriteLine("   text-align: left;")
$txtstream.WriteLine("   white-Space: nowrap;")
$txtstream.WriteLine("}")
$txtstream.WriteLine("span")
$txtstream.WriteLine("{")
$txtstream.WriteLine("   COLOR: white;")
$txtstream.WriteLine("   BACKGROUND-COLOR: navy;")
$txtstream.WriteLine("   FONT-FAMILY: font-family: Cambria, serif;")
$txtstream.WriteLine("   FONT-SIZE: 10px;")
$txtstream.WriteLine("   text-align: left;")
$txtstream.WriteLine("   white-Space: nowrap;")
$txtstream.WriteLine("   display:inline-block;")
$txtstream.WriteLine("   width: 100%;")
$txtstream.WriteLine("}")
$txtstream.WriteLine("textarea")
$txtstream.WriteLine("{")
$txtstream.WriteLine("   COLOR: white;")
$txtstream.WriteLine("   BACKGROUND-COLOR: navy;")
$txtstream.WriteLine("   FONT-FAMILY: font-family: Cambria, serif;")
$txtstream.WriteLine("   FONT-SIZE: 10px;")
$txtstream.WriteLine("   text-align: left;")
$txtstream.WriteLine("   white-Space: nowrap;")
$txtstream.WriteLine("   width: 100%;")
$txtstream.WriteLine("}")
```

```
$txtstream.WriteLine("select")
$txtstream.WriteLine("{")
$txtstream.WriteLine("    COLOR: white;")
$txtstream.WriteLine("    BACKGROUND-COLOR: navy;")
$txtstream.WriteLine("    FONT-FAMILY: font-family: Cambria, serif;")
$txtstream.WriteLine("    FONT-SIZE: 10px;")
$txtstream.WriteLine("    text-align: left;")
$txtstream.WriteLine("    white-Space: nowrap;")
$txtstream.WriteLine("    width: 100%;")
$txtstream.WriteLine("}")
$txtstream.WriteLine("input")
$txtstream.WriteLine("{")
$txtstream.WriteLine("    COLOR: white;")
$txtstream.WriteLine("    BACKGROUND-COLOR: navy;")
$txtstream.WriteLine("    FONT-FAMILY: font-family: Cambria, serif;")
$txtstream.WriteLine("    FONT-SIZE: 12px;")
$txtstream.WriteLine("    text-align: left;")
$txtstream.WriteLine("    display:table-cell;")
$txtstream.WriteLine("    white-Space: nowrap;")
$txtstream.WriteLine("}")
$txtstream.WriteLine("h1 {")
$txtstream.WriteLine("color: antiquewhite;")
$txtstream.WriteLine("text-shadow: 1px 1px 1px black;")
$txtstream.WriteLine("padding: 3px;")
$txtstream.WriteLine("text-align: center;")
$txtstream.WriteLine("box-shadow: inset 2px 2px 5px rgba(0,0,0,0.5), inset -2px -2px 5px rgba(255,255,255,0.5)")
$txtstream.WriteLine("}")
$txtstream.WriteLine("</style>")
```

OSCILLATING ROW COLORS

```
$txtstream.WriteLine("<style>")
$txtstream.WriteLine("th")
$txtstream.WriteLine("{")
$txtstream.WriteLine("   COLOR: white;")
$txtstream.WriteLine("   BACKGROUND-COLOR: navy;")
$txtstream.WriteLine("   FONT-FAMILY:font-family: Cambria, serif;")
$txtstream.WriteLine("   FONT-SIZE: 12px;")
$txtstream.WriteLine("   text-align: left;")
$txtstream.WriteLine("   white-Space: nowrap;")
$txtstream.WriteLine("}")
$txtstream.WriteLine("td")
$txtstream.WriteLine("{")
$txtstream.WriteLine("   COLOR: navy;")
$txtstream.WriteLine("   FONT-FAMILY: font-family: Cambria, serif;")
$txtstream.WriteLine("   FONT-SIZE: 12px;")
$txtstream.WriteLine("   text-align: left;")
$txtstream.WriteLine("   white-Space: nowrap;")
$txtstream.WriteLine("}")
$txtstream.WriteLine("div")
$txtstream.WriteLine("{")
$txtstream.WriteLine("   COLOR: navy;")
$txtstream.WriteLine("   FONT-FAMILY: font-family: Cambria, serif;")
$txtstream.WriteLine("   FONT-SIZE: 12px;")
$txtstream.WriteLine("   text-align: left;")
$txtstream.WriteLine("   white-Space: nowrap;")
$txtstream.WriteLine("}")
$txtstream.WriteLine("span")
$txtstream.WriteLine("{")
$txtstream.WriteLine("   COLOR: navy;")
$txtstream.WriteLine("   FONT-FAMILY: font-family: Cambria, serif;")
$txtstream.WriteLine("   FONT-SIZE: 12px;")
$txtstream.WriteLine("   text-align: left;")
```

```
$txtstream.WriteLine("   white-Space: nowrap;")
$txtstream.WriteLine("   width: 100%;")
$txtstream.WriteLine("}")
$txtstream.WriteLine("textarea")
$txtstream.WriteLine("{")
$txtstream.WriteLine("   COLOR: navy;")
$txtstream.WriteLine("   FONT-FAMILY: font-family: Cambria, serif;")
$txtstream.WriteLine("   FONT-SIZE: 12px;")
$txtstream.WriteLine("   text-align: left;")
$txtstream.WriteLine("   white-Space: nowrap;")
$txtstream.WriteLine("   display:inline-block;")
$txtstream.WriteLine("   width: 100%;")
$txtstream.WriteLine("}")
$txtstream.WriteLine("select")
$txtstream.WriteLine("{")
$txtstream.WriteLine("   COLOR: navy;")
$txtstream.WriteLine("   FONT-FAMILY: font-family: Cambria, serif;")
$txtstream.WriteLine("   FONT-SIZE: 10px;")
$txtstream.WriteLine("   text-align: left;")
$txtstream.WriteLine("   white-Space: nowrap;")
$txtstream.WriteLine("   display:inline-block;")
$txtstream.WriteLine("   width: 100%;")
$txtstream.WriteLine("}")
$txtstream.WriteLine("input")
$txtstream.WriteLine("{")
$txtstream.WriteLine("   COLOR: navy;")
$txtstream.WriteLine("   FONT-FAMILY: font-family: Cambria, serif;")
$txtstream.WriteLine("   FONT-SIZE: 12px;")
$txtstream.WriteLine("   text-align: left;")
$txtstream.WriteLine("   display:table-cell;")
$txtstream.WriteLine("   white-Space: nowrap;")
$txtstream.WriteLine("}")
$txtstream.WriteLine("h1 {")
```

```
$txtstream.WriteLine("color: antiquewhite;")
$txtstream.WriteLine("text-shadow: 1px 1px 1px black;")
$txtstream.WriteLine("padding: 3px;")
$txtstream.WriteLine("text-align: center;")
$txtstream.WriteLine("box-shadow: inset 2px 2px 5px rgba(0,0,0,0.5), inset -2px -2px 5px rgba(255,255,255,0.5)")
$txtstream.WriteLine("}")
$txtstream.WriteLine("tr:nth-child(even){background-color:#f2f2f2;}")
$txtstream.WriteLine("tr:nth-child(odd){background-color:#cccccc; color:#f2f2f2;}")
$txtstream.WriteLine("</style>")
```

GHOST DECORATED

```
$txtstream.WriteLine("<style type='text/css'>")
$txtstream.WriteLine("th")
$txtstream.WriteLine("{")
$txtstream.WriteLine("    COLOR: black;")
$txtstream.WriteLine("    BACKGROUND-COLOR: white;")
$txtstream.WriteLine("    FONT-FAMILY:font-family: Cambria, serif;")
$txtstream.WriteLine("    FONT-SIZE: 12px;")
$txtstream.WriteLine("    text-align: left;")
$txtstream.WriteLine("    white-Space: nowrap;")
$txtstream.WriteLine("}")
$txtstream.WriteLine("td")
$txtstream.WriteLine("{")
$txtstream.WriteLine("    COLOR: black;")
$txtstream.WriteLine("    BACKGROUND-COLOR: white;")
$txtstream.WriteLine("    FONT-FAMILY: font-family: Cambria, serif;")
$txtstream.WriteLine("    FONT-SIZE: 12px;")
$txtstream.WriteLine("    text-align: left;")
$txtstream.WriteLine("    white-Space: nowrap;")
$txtstream.WriteLine("}")
```

```
$txtstream.WriteLine("div")
$txtstream.WriteLine("{")
$txtstream.WriteLine("   COLOR: black;")
$txtstream.WriteLine("   BACKGROUND-COLOR: white;")
$txtstream.WriteLine("   FONT-FAMILY: font-family: Cambria, serif;")
$txtstream.WriteLine("   FONT-SIZE: 10px;")
$txtstream.WriteLine("   text-align: left;")
$txtstream.WriteLine("   white-Space: nowrap;")
$txtstream.WriteLine("}")
$txtstream.WriteLine("span")
$txtstream.WriteLine("{")
$txtstream.WriteLine("   COLOR: black;")
$txtstream.WriteLine("   BACKGROUND-COLOR: white;")
$txtstream.WriteLine("   FONT-FAMILY: font-family: Cambria, serif;")
$txtstream.WriteLine("   FONT-SIZE: 10px;")
$txtstream.WriteLine("   text-align: left;")
$txtstream.WriteLine("   white-Space: nowrap;")
$txtstream.WriteLine("   display:inline-block;")
$txtstream.WriteLine("   width: 100%;")
$txtstream.WriteLine("}")
$txtstream.WriteLine("textarea")
$txtstream.WriteLine("{")
$txtstream.WriteLine("   COLOR: black;")
$txtstream.WriteLine("   BACKGROUND-COLOR: white;")
$txtstream.WriteLine("   FONT-FAMILY: font-family: Cambria, serif;")
$txtstream.WriteLine("   FONT-SIZE: 10px;")
$txtstream.WriteLine("   text-align: left;")
$txtstream.WriteLine("   white-Space: nowrap;")
$txtstream.WriteLine("   width: 100%;")
$txtstream.WriteLine("}")
$txtstream.WriteLine("select")
$txtstream.WriteLine("{")
$txtstream.WriteLine("   COLOR: black;")
```

```
$txtstream.WriteLine("   BACKGROUND-COLOR: white;")
$txtstream.WriteLine("   FONT-FAMILY: font-family: Cambria, serif;")
$txtstream.WriteLine("   FONT-SIZE: 10px;")
$txtstream.WriteLine("   text-align: left;")
$txtstream.WriteLine("   white-Space: nowrap;")
$txtstream.WriteLine("   width: 100%;")
$txtstream.WriteLine("}")
$txtstream.WriteLine("input")
$txtstream.WriteLine("{")
$txtstream.WriteLine("   COLOR: black;")
$txtstream.WriteLine("   BACKGROUND-COLOR: white;")
$txtstream.WriteLine("   FONT-FAMILY: font-family: Cambria, serif;")
$txtstream.WriteLine("   FONT-SIZE: 12px;")
$txtstream.WriteLine("   text-align: left;")
$txtstream.WriteLine("   display:table-cell;")
$txtstream.WriteLine("   white-Space: nowrap;")
$txtstream.WriteLine("}")
$txtstream.WriteLine("h1 {")
$txtstream.WriteLine("color: antiquewhite;")
$txtstream.WriteLine("text-shadow: 1px 1px 1px black;")
$txtstream.WriteLine("padding: 3px;")
$txtstream.WriteLine("text-align: center;")
$txtstream.WriteLine("box-shadow: inset 2px 2px 5px rgba(0,0,0,0.5), inset -
2px -2px 5px rgba(255,255,255,0.5)")
$txtstream.WriteLine("}")
$txtstream.WriteLine("</style>")
```

3D

```
$txtstream.WriteLine("<style type='text/css'>")
$txtstream.WriteLine("body")
$txtstream.WriteLine("{")
```

```
$txtstream.WriteLine("    PADDING-RIGHT: 0px;")
$txtstream.WriteLine("    PADDING-LEFT: 0px;")
$txtstream.WriteLine("    PADDING-BOTTOM: 0px;")
$txtstream.WriteLine("    MARGIN: 0px;")
$txtstream.WriteLine("    COLOR: #333;")
$txtstream.WriteLine("    PADDING-TOP: 0px;")
$txtstream.WriteLine("    FONT-FAMILY: verdana, arial, helvetica, sans-
serif;")
$txtstream.WriteLine("}")
$txtstream.WriteLine("table")
$txtstream.WriteLine("{")
$txtstream.WriteLine("    BORDER-RIGHT: #999999 3px solid;")
$txtstream.WriteLine("    PADDING-RIGHT: 6px;")
$txtstream.WriteLine("    PADDING-LEFT: 6px;")
$txtstream.WriteLine("    FONT-WEIGHT: Bold;")
$txtstream.WriteLine("    FONT-SIZE: 14px;")
$txtstream.WriteLine("    PADDING-BOTTOM: 6px;")
$txtstream.WriteLine("    COLOR: Peru;")
$txtstream.WriteLine("    LINE-HEIGHT: 14px;")
$txtstream.WriteLine("    PADDING-TOP: 6px;")
$txtstream.WriteLine("    BORDER-BOTTOM: #999 1px solid;")
$txtstream.WriteLine("    BACKGROUND-COLOR: #eeeeee;")
$txtstream.WriteLine("    FONT-FAMILY: verdana, arial, helvetica, sans-
serif;")
$txtstream.WriteLine("    FONT-SIZE: 12px;")
$txtstream.WriteLine("}")
$txtstream.WriteLine("th")
$txtstream.WriteLine("{")
$txtstream.WriteLine("    BORDER-RIGHT: #999999 3px solid;")
$txtstream.WriteLine("    PADDING-RIGHT: 6px;")
$txtstream.WriteLine("    PADDING-LEFT: 6px;")
$txtstream.WriteLine("    FONT-WEIGHT: Bold;")
$txtstream.WriteLine("    FONT-SIZE: 14px;")
```

```
$txtstream.WriteLine("   PADDING-BOTTOM: 6px;")
$txtstream.WriteLine("   COLOR: darkred;")
$txtstream.WriteLine("   LINE-HEIGHT: 14px;")
$txtstream.WriteLine("   PADDING-TOP: 6px;")
$txtstream.WriteLine("   BORDER-BOTTOM: #999 1px solid;")
$txtstream.WriteLine("   BACKGROUND-COLOR: #eeeeee;")
$txtstream.WriteLine("   FONT-FAMILY:font-family: Cambria, serif;")
$txtstream.WriteLine("   FONT-SIZE: 12px;")
$txtstream.WriteLine("   text-align: left;")
$txtstream.WriteLine("   white-Space: nowrap;")
$txtstream.WriteLine("}")
$txtstream.WriteLine(".th")
$txtstream.WriteLine("{")
$txtstream.WriteLine("   BORDER-RIGHT: #999999 2px solid;")
$txtstream.WriteLine("   PADDING-RIGHT: 6px;")
$txtstream.WriteLine("   PADDING-LEFT: 6px;")
$txtstream.WriteLine("   FONT-WEIGHT: Bold;")
$txtstream.WriteLine("   PADDING-BOTTOM: 6px;")
$txtstream.WriteLine("   COLOR: black;")
$txtstream.WriteLine("   PADDING-TOP: 6px;")
$txtstream.WriteLine("   BORDER-BOTTOM: #999 2px solid;")
$txtstream.WriteLine("   BACKGROUND-COLOR: #eeeeee;")
$txtstream.WriteLine("   FONT-FAMILY: font-family: Cambria, serif;")
$txtstream.WriteLine("   FONT-SIZE: 10px;")
$txtstream.WriteLine("   text-align: right;")
$txtstream.WriteLine("   white-Space: nowrap;")
$txtstream.WriteLine("}")
$txtstream.WriteLine("td")
$txtstream.WriteLine("{")
$txtstream.WriteLine("   BORDER-RIGHT: #999999 3px solid;")
$txtstream.WriteLine("   PADDING-RIGHT: 6px;")
$txtstream.WriteLine("   PADDING-LEFT: 6px;")
$txtstream.WriteLine("   FONT-WEIGHT: Normal;")
```

```
$txtstream.WriteLine("   PADDING-BOTTOM: 6px;")
$txtstream.WriteLine("   COLOR: navy;")
$txtstream.WriteLine("   LINE-HEIGHT: 14px;")
$txtstream.WriteLine("   PADDING-TOP: 6px;")
$txtstream.WriteLine("   BORDER-BOTTOM: #999 1px solid;")
$txtstream.WriteLine("   BACKGROUND-COLOR: #eeeeee;")
$txtstream.WriteLine("   FONT-FAMILY: font-family: Cambria, serif;")
$txtstream.WriteLine("   FONT-SIZE: 12px;")
$txtstream.WriteLine("   text-align: left;")
$txtstream.WriteLine("   white-Space: nowrap;")
$txtstream.WriteLine("}")
$txtstream.WriteLine("div")
$txtstream.WriteLine("{")
$txtstream.WriteLine("   BORDER-RIGHT: #999999 3px solid;")
$txtstream.WriteLine("   PADDING-RIGHT: 6px;")
$txtstream.WriteLine("   PADDING-LEFT: 6px;")
$txtstream.WriteLine("   FONT-WEIGHT: Normal;")
$txtstream.WriteLine("   PADDING-BOTTOM: 6px;")
$txtstream.WriteLine("   COLOR: white;")
$txtstream.WriteLine("   PADDING-TOP: 6px;")
$txtstream.WriteLine("   BORDER-BOTTOM: #999 1px solid;")
$txtstream.WriteLine("   BACKGROUND-COLOR: navy;")
$txtstream.WriteLine("   FONT-FAMILY: font-family: Cambria, serif;")
$txtstream.WriteLine("   FONT-SIZE: 10px;")
$txtstream.WriteLine("   text-align: left;")
$txtstream.WriteLine("   white-Space: nowrap;")
$txtstream.WriteLine("}")
$txtstream.WriteLine("span")
$txtstream.WriteLine("{")
$txtstream.WriteLine("   BORDER-RIGHT: #999999 3px solid;")
$txtstream.WriteLine("   PADDING-RIGHT: 3px;")
$txtstream.WriteLine("   PADDING-LEFT: 3px;")
$txtstream.WriteLine("   FONT-WEIGHT: Normal;")
```

```
$txtstream.WriteLine("    PADDING-BOTTOM: 3px;")
$txtstream.WriteLine("    COLOR: white;")
$txtstream.WriteLine("    PADDING-TOP: 3px;")
$txtstream.WriteLine("    BORDER-BOTTOM: #999 1px solid;")
$txtstream.WriteLine("    BACKGROUND-COLOR: navy;")
$txtstream.WriteLine("    FONT-FAMILY: font-family: Cambria, serif;")
$txtstream.WriteLine("    FONT-SIZE: 10px;")
$txtstream.WriteLine("    text-align: left;")
$txtstream.WriteLine("    white-Space: nowrap;")
$txtstream.WriteLine("    display:inline-block;")
$txtstream.WriteLine("    width: 100%;")
$txtstream.WriteLine("}")
$txtstream.WriteLine("textarea")
$txtstream.WriteLine("{")
$txtstream.WriteLine("    BORDER-RIGHT: #999999 3px solid;")
$txtstream.WriteLine("    PADDING-RIGHT: 3px;")
$txtstream.WriteLine("    PADDING-LEFT: 3px;")
$txtstream.WriteLine("    FONT-WEIGHT: Normal;")
$txtstream.WriteLine("    PADDING-BOTTOM: 3px;")
$txtstream.WriteLine("    COLOR: white;")
$txtstream.WriteLine("    PADDING-TOP: 3px;")
$txtstream.WriteLine("    BORDER-BOTTOM: #999 1px solid;")
$txtstream.WriteLine("    BACKGROUND-COLOR: navy;")
$txtstream.WriteLine("    FONT-FAMILY: font-family: Cambria, serif;")
$txtstream.WriteLine("    FONT-SIZE: 10px;")
$txtstream.WriteLine("    text-align: left;")
$txtstream.WriteLine("    white-Space: nowrap;")
$txtstream.WriteLine("    width: 100%;")
$txtstream.WriteLine("}")
$txtstream.WriteLine("select")
$txtstream.WriteLine("{")
$txtstream.WriteLine("    BORDER-RIGHT: #999999 3px solid;")
$txtstream.WriteLine("    PADDING-RIGHT: 6px;")
```

```
$txtstream.WriteLine("   PADDING-LEFT: 6px;")
$txtstream.WriteLine("   FONT-WEIGHT: Normal;")
$txtstream.WriteLine("   PADDING-BOTTOM: 6px;")
$txtstream.WriteLine("   COLOR: white;")
$txtstream.WriteLine("   PADDING-TOP: 6px;")
$txtstream.WriteLine("   BORDER-BOTTOM: #999 1px solid;")
$txtstream.WriteLine("   BACKGROUND-COLOR: navy;")
$txtstream.WriteLine("   FONT-FAMILY: font-family: Cambria, serif;")
$txtstream.WriteLine("   FONT-SIZE: 10px;")
$txtstream.WriteLine("   text-align: left;")
$txtstream.WriteLine("   white-Space: nowrap;")
$txtstream.WriteLine("   width: 100%;")
$txtstream.WriteLine("}")
$txtstream.WriteLine("input")
$txtstream.WriteLine("{")
$txtstream.WriteLine("   BORDER-RIGHT: #999999 3px solid;")
$txtstream.WriteLine("   PADDING-RIGHT: 3px;")
$txtstream.WriteLine("   PADDING-LEFT: 3px;")
$txtstream.WriteLine("   FONT-WEIGHT: Bold;")
$txtstream.WriteLine("   PADDING-BOTTOM: 3px;")
$txtstream.WriteLine("   COLOR: white;")
$txtstream.WriteLine("   PADDING-TOP: 3px;")
$txtstream.WriteLine("   BORDER-BOTTOM: #999 1px solid;")
$txtstream.WriteLine("   BACKGROUND-COLOR: navy;")
$txtstream.WriteLine("   FONT-FAMILY: font-family: Cambria, serif;")
$txtstream.WriteLine("   FONT-SIZE: 12px;")
$txtstream.WriteLine("   text-align: left;")
$txtstream.WriteLine("   display:table-cell;")
$txtstream.WriteLine("   white-Space: nowrap;")
$txtstream.WriteLine("   width: 100%;")
$txtstream.WriteLine("}")
$txtstream.WriteLine("h1 {")
$txtstream.WriteLine("color: antiquewhite;")
```

```
$txtstream.WriteLine("text-shadow: 1px 1px 1px black;")
$txtstream.WriteLine("padding: 3px;")
$txtstream.WriteLine("text-align: center;")
$txtstream.WriteLine("box-shadow: inset 2px 2px 5px rgba(0,0,0,0.5), inset -
2px -2px 5px rgba(255,255,255,0.5)")
$txtstream.WriteLine("}")
$txtstream.WriteLine("</style>")
```

SHADOW BOX

```
$txtstream.WriteLine("<style type='text/css'>")
$txtstream.WriteLine("body")
$txtstream.WriteLine("{")
$txtstream.WriteLine("   PADDING-RIGHT: 0px;")
$txtstream.WriteLine("   PADDING-LEFT: 0px;")
$txtstream.WriteLine("   PADDING-BOTTOM: 0px;")
$txtstream.WriteLine("   MARGIN: 0px;")
$txtstream.WriteLine("   COLOR: #333;")
$txtstream.WriteLine("   PADDING-TOP: 0px;")
$txtstream.WriteLine("   FONT-FAMILY: verdana, arial, helvetica, sans-
serif;")
$txtstream.WriteLine("}")
$txtstream.WriteLine("table")
$txtstream.WriteLine("{")
$txtstream.WriteLine("   BORDER-RIGHT: #999999 1px solid;")
$txtstream.WriteLine("   PADDING-RIGHT: 1px;")
$txtstream.WriteLine("   PADDING-LEFT: 1px;")
$txtstream.WriteLine("   PADDING-BOTTOM: 1px;")
$txtstream.WriteLine("   LINE-HEIGHT: 8px;")
$txtstream.WriteLine("   PADDING-TOP: 1px;")
$txtstream.WriteLine("   BORDER-BOTTOM: #999 1px solid;")
$txtstream.WriteLine("   BACKGROUND-COLOR: #eeeeee;")
```

$txtstream.WriteLine("
filter:progid:DXImageTransform.Microsoft.Shadow(color='silver', Direction=135, Strength=16)")
$txtstream.WriteLine("}")
$txtstream.WriteLine("th")
$txtstream.WriteLine("{")
$txtstream.WriteLine("   BORDER-RIGHT: #999999 3px solid;")
$txtstream.WriteLine("   PADDING-RIGHT: 6px;")
$txtstream.WriteLine("   PADDING-LEFT: 6px;")
$txtstream.WriteLine("   FONT-WEIGHT: Bold;")
$txtstream.WriteLine("   FONT-SIZE: 14px;")
$txtstream.WriteLine("   PADDING-BOTTOM: 6px;")
$txtstream.WriteLine("   COLOR: darkred;")
$txtstream.WriteLine("   LINE-HEIGHT: 14px;")
$txtstream.WriteLine("   PADDING-TOP: 6px;")
$txtstream.WriteLine("   BORDER-BOTTOM: #999 1px solid;")
$txtstream.WriteLine("   BACKGROUND-COLOR: #eeeeee;")
$txtstream.WriteLine("   FONT-FAMILY: font-family: Cambria, serif;")
$txtstream.WriteLine("   FONT-SIZE: 12px;")
$txtstream.WriteLine("   text-align: left;")
$txtstream.WriteLine("   white-Space: nowrap;")
$txtstream.WriteLine("}")
$txtstream.WriteLine(".th")
$txtstream.WriteLine("{")
$txtstream.WriteLine("   BORDER-RIGHT: #999999 2px solid;")
$txtstream.WriteLine("   PADDING-RIGHT: 6px;")
$txtstream.WriteLine("   PADDING-LEFT: 6px;")
$txtstream.WriteLine("   FONT-WEIGHT: Bold;")
$txtstream.WriteLine("   PADDING-BOTTOM: 6px;")
$txtstream.WriteLine("   COLOR: black;")
$txtstream.WriteLine("   PADDING-TOP: 6px;")
$txtstream.WriteLine("   BORDER-BOTTOM: #999 2px solid;")
$txtstream.WriteLine("   BACKGROUND-COLOR: #eeeeee;")

$txtstream.WriteLine("   FONT-FAMILY: font-family: Cambria, serif;")

$txtstream.WriteLine("   FONT-SIZE: 10px;")

$txtstream.WriteLine("   text-align: right;")

$txtstream.WriteLine("   white-Space: nowrap;")

$txtstream.WriteLine("}")

$txtstream.WriteLine("td")

$txtstream.WriteLine("{")

$txtstream.WriteLine("   BORDER-RIGHT: #999999 3px solid;")

$txtstream.WriteLine("   PADDING-RIGHT: 6px;")

$txtstream.WriteLine("   PADDING-LEFT: 6px;")

$txtstream.WriteLine("   FONT-WEIGHT: Normal;")

$txtstream.WriteLine("   PADDING-BOTTOM: 6px;")

$txtstream.WriteLine("   COLOR: navy;")

$txtstream.WriteLine("   LINE-HEIGHT: 14px;")

$txtstream.WriteLine("   PADDING-TOP: 6px;")

$txtstream.WriteLine("   BORDER-BOTTOM: #999 1px solid;")

$txtstream.WriteLine("   BACKGROUND-COLOR: #eeeeee;")

$txtstream.WriteLine("   FONT-FAMILY: font-family: Cambria, serif;")

$txtstream.WriteLine("   FONT-SIZE: 12px;")

$txtstream.WriteLine("   text-align: left;")

$txtstream.WriteLine("   white-Space: nowrap;")

$txtstream.WriteLine("}")

$txtstream.WriteLine("div")

$txtstream.WriteLine("{")

$txtstream.WriteLine("   BORDER-RIGHT: #999999 3px solid;")

$txtstream.WriteLine("   PADDING-RIGHT: 6px;")

$txtstream.WriteLine("   PADDING-LEFT: 6px;")

$txtstream.WriteLine("   FONT-WEIGHT: Normal;")

$txtstream.WriteLine("   PADDING-BOTTOM: 6px;")

$txtstream.WriteLine("   COLOR: white;")

$txtstream.WriteLine("   PADDING-TOP: 6px;")

$txtstream.WriteLine("   BORDER-BOTTOM: #999 1px solid;")

$txtstream.WriteLine("   BACKGROUND-COLOR: navy;")

```
$txtstream.WriteLine("   FONT-FAMILY: font-family: Cambria, serif;")
$txtstream.WriteLine("   FONT-SIZE: 10px;")
$txtstream.WriteLine("   text-align: left;")
$txtstream.WriteLine("   white-Space: nowrap;")
$txtstream.WriteLine("}")
$txtstream.WriteLine("span")
$txtstream.WriteLine("{")
$txtstream.WriteLine("   BORDER-RIGHT: #999999 3px solid;")
$txtstream.WriteLine("   PADDING-RIGHT: 3px;")
$txtstream.WriteLine("   PADDING-LEFT: 3px;")
$txtstream.WriteLine("   FONT-WEIGHT: Normal;")
$txtstream.WriteLine("   PADDING-BOTTOM: 3px;")
$txtstream.WriteLine("   COLOR: white;")
$txtstream.WriteLine("   PADDING-TOP: 3px;")
$txtstream.WriteLine("   BORDER-BOTTOM: #999 1px solid;")
$txtstream.WriteLine("   BACKGROUND-COLOR: navy;")
$txtstream.WriteLine("   FONT-FAMILY: font-family: Cambria, serif;")
$txtstream.WriteLine("   FONT-SIZE: 10px;")
$txtstream.WriteLine("   text-align: left;")
$txtstream.WriteLine("   white-Space: nowrap;")
$txtstream.WriteLine("   display: inline-block;")
$txtstream.WriteLine("   width: 100%;")
$txtstream.WriteLine("}")
$txtstream.WriteLine("textarea")
$txtstream.WriteLine("{")
$txtstream.WriteLine("   BORDER-RIGHT: #999999 3px solid;")
$txtstream.WriteLine("   PADDING-RIGHT: 3px;")
$txtstream.WriteLine("   PADDING-LEFT: 3px;")
$txtstream.WriteLine("   FONT-WEIGHT: Normal;")
$txtstream.WriteLine("   PADDING-BOTTOM: 3px;")
$txtstream.WriteLine("   COLOR: white;")
$txtstream.WriteLine("   PADDING-TOP: 3px;")
$txtstream.WriteLine("   BORDER-BOTTOM: #999 1px solid;")
```

```
$txtstream.WriteLine("   BACKGROUND-COLOR: navy;")
$txtstream.WriteLine("   FONT-FAMILY: font-family: Cambria, serif;")
$txtstream.WriteLine("   FONT-SIZE: 10px;")
$txtstream.WriteLine("   text-align: left;")
$txtstream.WriteLine("   white-Space: nowrap;")
$txtstream.WriteLine("   width: 100%;")
$txtstream.WriteLine("}")
$txtstream.WriteLine("select")
$txtstream.WriteLine("{")
$txtstream.WriteLine("   BORDER-RIGHT: #999999 3px solid;")
$txtstream.WriteLine("   PADDING-RIGHT: 6px;")
$txtstream.WriteLine("   PADDING-LEFT: 6px;")
$txtstream.WriteLine("   FONT-WEIGHT: Normal;")
$txtstream.WriteLine("   PADDING-BOTTOM: 6px;")
$txtstream.WriteLine("   COLOR: white;")
$txtstream.WriteLine("   PADDING-TOP: 6px;")
$txtstream.WriteLine("   BORDER-BOTTOM: #999 1px solid;")
$txtstream.WriteLine("   BACKGROUND-COLOR: navy;")
$txtstream.WriteLine("   FONT-FAMILY: font-family: Cambria, serif;")
$txtstream.WriteLine("   FONT-SIZE: 10px;")
$txtstream.WriteLine("   text-align: left;")
$txtstream.WriteLine("   white-Space: nowrap;")
$txtstream.WriteLine("   width: 100%;")
$txtstream.WriteLine("}")
$txtstream.WriteLine("input")
$txtstream.WriteLine("{")
$txtstream.WriteLine("   BORDER-RIGHT: #999999 3px solid;")
$txtstream.WriteLine("   PADDING-RIGHT: 3px;")
$txtstream.WriteLine("   PADDING-LEFT: 3px;")
$txtstream.WriteLine("   FONT-WEIGHT: Bold;")
$txtstream.WriteLine("   PADDING-BOTTOM: 3px;")
$txtstream.WriteLine("   COLOR: white;")
$txtstream.WriteLine("   PADDING-TOP: 3px;")
```

```
$txtstream.WriteLine("    BORDER-BOTTOM: #999 1px solid;")
$txtstream.WriteLine("    BACKGROUND-COLOR: navy;")
$txtstream.WriteLine("    FONT-FAMILY: font-family: Cambria, serif;")
$txtstream.WriteLine("    FONT-SIZE: 12px;")
$txtstream.WriteLine("    text-align: left;")
$txtstream.WriteLine("    display: table-cell;")
$txtstream.WriteLine("    white-Space: nowrap;")
$txtstream.WriteLine("    width: 100%;")
$txtstream.WriteLine("}")
$txtstream.WriteLine("h1 {")
$txtstream.WriteLine("color: antiquewhite;")
$txtstream.WriteLine("text-shadow: 1px 1px 1px black;")
$txtstream.WriteLine("padding: 3px;")
$txtstream.WriteLine("text-align: center;")
$txtstream.WriteLine("box-shadow: inset 2px 2px 5px rgba(0,0,0,0.5), inset -2px -2px 5px rgba(255,255,255,0.5)")
$txtstream.WriteLine("}")
$txtstream.WriteLine("</style>")
```